THE INSTITUTE *for*
LUXURY HOME
MARKETING

Happy New Year!

Here at last is the Second Edition of *Rich Buyer,
Rich Seller: The Real Estate Agents' Updated Guide to
Marketing Luxury Homes.*

This new book contains current statistics and lots of
new ideas. I hope you will find it useful as you plan
and implement your 2008 marketing strategies.

Best wishes for great success,

Laurie Moore-Moore

Rich Buyer, Rich Seller!

The Real Estate Agents' updated Guide to Marketing Luxury Homes

Expanded Second Edition

Laurie Moore-Moore
Founder
The Institute for Luxury Home Marketing

Book design and production by RFE Enterprises, Inc.

Printed in the United States of America

Library of Congress Cataloging-in-Publication Data
On file with the Publisher

ISBN 0-9726001-1-6

Institute for Luxury Home Marketing
1409 South Lamar # 215
Dallas, Texas 75215-6814
214-485-3000

Dedication

For the two men who make my life richer
by their presence

Roger, the love of my life
Waco, our wonderful son who always makes us proud

Contents

Introduction

More than 10,000 copies of the original "Rich Buyer, Rich Seller! The Real Estate Agents' Guide to Marketing Luxury Homes" have found their way into the hands of real estate professionals since this book was introduced at the very end of 2002

Since then, the luxury home market has grown by leaps and bounds – as has the number of real estate agents and brokers pursuing this lucrative segment. Competition is fierce. Now, more than ever, you need information and ideas to help you position yourself as a luxury home expert.

If your goal is to understand and meet the needs
of affluent homebuyers and sellers,
*this **newly-revised and expanded book** is for YOU.*

This book begins with information gathering about the upper-tier market, about affluent prospects, about your competitors, and about the skills you need to work with the affluent. I believe if you are knowledgeable about these things, you enhance your probability of success. There are also lots of marketing ideas and tips for helping you secure the upper-priced listing, capture buyer prospects, and sell properties. I hope you will enjoy reading this book and find it to be a useful tool as you work with rich buyers, rich sellers, and ultra consumers.

May your real estate successes bring you happiness and affluence,

Laurie Moore-Moore
Founder
The Institute for Luxury Home Marketing
www.LuxuryHomeMarketing.com   www.CLHMS.com

P.S. Some copies of the original edition of this book were actually sold on e-Bay for as much as $125. Don't buy your copy there! Instead, find it for a lot less on our Website, www.Luxury HomeMarketing.com.

Chapter One

The Importance of Information Gathering

Over the past ten years I've trained more than 12,000 agents in luxury home marketing. Invariably, agents tell me that two of the stories that I share in my presentations are important in reinforcing the critical importance of information gathering for success. So, I decided to share them with you as well.

Story One

I've learned a lot about business from my young nephew. When he was born he was named Paul Powell IV. His dad is Paul Powell III and we call his dad P3. So, the obvious name for this new little guy was P4. We called this child P4 for about three years and then it became readily apparent that this was not the right name for him. P4 was a going concern; he was into everything; he never slowed down; he had a zillion questions. He was turbo-charged. So we began to call him Turbo.

One day when Turbo was not quite four years old, he was outside with his dad. It was a hot Texas summer day and they were working on a father-and-son project – washing the car. The dad, P3, was soaping away and Turbo's job was rinsing the car with the hose.

If you've been around a three- or a four-year-old, you know the attention span is short. Sure enough, it wasn't long before Turbo became bored rinsing the car. He spun around and began to water a flowerbed where nothing was planted yet, just freshly turned soil. After about a minute, a frog popped up. Turbo's eyes got really big. He turned around to his dad and said, "Dad, I just made a frog!" His dad laughed and went on soaping the car. Meanwhile, Turbo began watering the flower bed with a vengeance and it didn't take very long before POP! POP! up popped two more frogs. Turbo turned back around and said, "Dad, I made two more frogs and it's easy: all you do is add water to dirt."

This is a silly story. But when I heard it, I thought, "I've done that." I've done it more than once in my own business, and I'll bet you have too: We jump to the wrong conclusion because we don't have all the information. Turbo didn't know that in the hot Texas summer frogs burrow down into the ground to stay cool. It was the water that provided the impetus for those frogs to pop right up, but, because Turbo didn't have all the information, he mistakenly thought he'd made frogs.

Think about that in the context of your own real estate business. When you first came into real estate, did you step back and gather information and analyze the market to determine which market segments in which areas were the most active, or did you just jump in and start doing business? Most of us simply begin with little or no information gathering. And, after you've been at this business for several years, there's the temptation to think, "I understand this business; I've been doing it a long time."

But, as you know, the market changes.

Story Two

If you were in real estate in 1981, you witnessed significant changes in the industry. Interest rates soared – eighteen, nineteen, twenty percent rates were common – and in most markets, housing demand dwindled. In Dallas, rates were high but the market had so much corporate growth, including a couple of major corporate group moves, that real estate activity was high. Because Dallas was one of the few active residential real estate markets in the country in 1981, the money came to Dallas. The investors, lenders, builders, and developers swarmed into the market. If you could spell "builder," you could be one. If you could show you knew which end of the hammer to hold, you probably had savings and loan institutions or other investors lined up to joint venture with you. As a result, new home inventory exploded.

But it wasn't long before the group moves were over and corporate activity began to slow as corporations began to downsize (or "right-size" as they prefer to call it). The oil industry cratered (oil is a small percentage of Dallas' economy, but at that point any healthy business would have helped). Suddenly real estate agents looked at the market and said, "Uh oh, we're going to have to tighten our belts, because times are going to be tough for a while in real estate in Dallas." The signs were there: Inventory was up and demand was down.

However, there was a real estate agent in Dallas who looked around and said, "You know, I've been doing this a long time, and if I've learned anything, it's that no matter what goes on in the market, there's always an opportunity. The trick is finding it." So she began to do a little information gathering. She analyzed the market and said to herself, "I think I see the opportunities. All these builders of all these speculatively built new homes are not going to be able to sell them. There are going to be savings and loans, mortgage companies, and other investors foreclosing on those properties. Institutions don't want to hold homes in their portfolios."

Then she realized, "I've handled a lot of new homes, I under-stand the new home product and I've worked with a lot of third party companies so I understand the institutional seller. I must be a new homes institutional expert." She began to go around and call on the S&Ls. She would tell them, "I know you're get-ting ready to foreclose on some new homes. You don't want to hold those homes in your portfolio. Call me; I can help you sell them. I'm a new homes institutional expert."

In the first twelve months of pursuing this strategy, she sold and closed more than $30 million worth of residential real estate. That's not a shabby number in any market. When others were complaining about their worst year in real estate, the agent who took the time to gather information found the opportunity for tremendous success.

This story is important for two reasons. First, it is a reminder that no matter what happens in the market there is always an opportunity. Second, it highlights (like Turbo and the frog) the importance of information gathering. One goal of this book is to help you gather the information and ideas that will help you be successful in luxury home marketing.

Chapter Two
Why Work in the Upper Tier?

Working in the upper tier has its advantages

There's a higher income potential. Since commission is based on a percentage of the selling price, a more expensive property generates a higher professional fee.

There are fewer competitors in the upper tier. Many agents are intimidated by the idea of working with the wealthy. They say, "I just don't know if I'd be comfortable working with somebody who lives in a million-dollar house." Money, power, and fame can be intimidating, and that keeps some agents out of the luxury home arena.

The upper-tier buyer or seller is often more resistant to economic change than prospects in the average price range. The wealthy are often less affected by fluctuations in interest rates and the vagaries of the economy. Many times they're all-cash buyers. Some are sophisticated investors who understand the real estate market and may invest in homes as part of their overall investment strategy.

National Association of Realtors' Research Economist Kevin Thorpe explained the upper-tier's usual resilience in an article entitled "Home Buying Trends—High-end Homes," in the

April 2001 issue of Real Estate Outlook. "Those in the higher income bracket generally look to buy pricier homes, and given their financial stability, are less sensitive to economic down-cycles. In addition, volatility in the stock market prompted many wealthy investors to turn to the real estate sector to add stability to their portfolio." Thorpe's comment remains true today in the highest income and net worth brackets, but is bit less true at the entry points of the luxury market.

The housing market in 2006 illustrated the resilience of the very wealthy consumer. Overall market sales (based on number of homes) slipped 10.8% in 2006, compared to the previous year. On the other hand, sales for homes priced at $5 million and above grew 18%. One thing did make that market slowdown (which gained traction throughout 2007) different from most previous slowdowns. There was more softening than would usually be expected in the bottom half of the luxury market.

This market decline was partly the result of what one pundit refers to as NINJA loans – loans made to those with No Income, No Job or Assets. It is true that many marginally qualified buyers stretched to buy luxury homes in the first few years of this century. Some lenders encouraged this by offering loans which defied traditional "good" lending practices. As a result, some luxury home owners had difficulty making their loan payments as these loans ballooned or rates clicked up. When lending practices tightened and some loans had significant rate adjustments, there were fewer qualified buyers and more available inventory, so the entry level of the upper-tier softened somewhat more than in past slow cycles.

Aggravating this was great deal of speculation in residential real estate. For example, in 2005, 40% of all homebuyers nationally were investors or second home buyers. This percentage dropped slightly in 2006, due to a reduction in the number of investors. The investors, many of whom were not buying based on market fundamentals, but were speculators, drove up both the level of sales and the prices. This created unsustainable "booms" in certain markets – including much of California and Florida, Phoenix-Scottsdale and Las Vegas. As these markets cooled, even segments of the luxury home market were affected. Demand slipped and prices softened.

But real estate remains an attractive investment for the wealthy. Merrill Lynch and CapGemini's World Wealth Report, released in June of 2007, reports that individuals around the world with $1 million or more in investable assets have 24% of their investment portfolios in direct or indirect real estate investments. What's even more positive for the real estate industry is that half of the wealthy's real estate investment is in residential property (excluding primary residences).

There is a great deal of personal satisfaction associated with being a successful agent in the upper tier. If you're successful in the luxury market, you probably have knowledge and competencies over and above those of the average agent. It can be satisfying to know you have solid skills.

Your peers recognize that to succeed in the higher price ranges, you have to be good. So, peer recognition or status is often associated with being successful in the luxury home market.

The luxury market offers challenges, too

Although there are lots of positives associated with targeting the luxury home niche, you must also recognize some not-so-positive realities.

Not every upper-tier listing sells. In fact, as price goes up, conversion tends to go down. So, there's a risk involved for the agent who must invest time and money in marketing each upper-tier listing.

Expensive homes usually take longer to sell. That adds to the risk. Be sure to educate your seller regarding expected sales time or days-on-market based on the property price.

It costs more to market an expensive property. The marketing plan required to give an upper priced property the targeted exposure necessary to sell it can be expensive. High quality brochures, targeted mailing lists, regional or national media exposure, special open house events, property-specific Web pages, and other marketing tools require a significant marketing budget. Generally, you expect to invest more to sell a fine home or estate property. Marketing time is also an issue since a longer sales period may mean more marketing dollars spent. Creativity and good networking will help you keep marketing costs affordable.

You are dealing with some of the most demanding buyers and sellers. You have to be prepared to communicate effectively and deliver high quality customer service. To be successful in the luxury home market, you have to be knowledgeable and skillful. You must know your market, understand the buying/selling process, and be committed to delivering quality customer service. You must take the time to understand your clients' wants and needs and clarify their expectations. Let them know how you work, what expectations you have of them, and what to expect from the home buying or selling process. Then, educate them about the market, keep communication open, and deal with problems promptly. After the fact, ask for a service evaluation to measure how well you did. And, don't forget to ask for testimonials and referrals.

Also recognize that these high-expectation buyers and sellers usually are not measuring your service based on the service of other real estate professionals. They are comparing your service to the service received from their professional shopper at Saks Fifth Avenue, the service enjoyed during their last stay at the Ritz Carlton Hotel, or the service delivered when they took a Crystal Cruise. In short, they are comparing how they felt about you and your service with the services of other purveyors of luxury products and services. Can you measure up?

Although you'll encounter fewer competitors in the high price ranges, the agents you are competing with are good, so competition is keen. Your skills need to be sharp if you expect to be competitive.

Sometimes expensive homes result in more complex transactions. Occasionally they're easier -- an all-cash transaction can sometimes be simple. But other players sometimes appear when you work in the upper tier. These other players can add complexity. Here's an example.

In the Midwest not long ago I was talking to a real estate salesperson who said, "Laurie, I just did the most complex listing presentation that I've ever done."

I asked, "What made it complex?"

"Well first of all," he said, "although the home is located here in my city in the Midwest, I did the listing presentation in the board room of a skyscraper in Manhattan, using my laptop and an LCD projector."

This made me curious, "Why did you have to do that?"

"The woman who owned the home died and the property went into a family trust," he told me. "Attending the listing presentation in New York were the following – the New York-based trustee, the family banker, the family accountant, heir number one and his spouse, heir number two and her business manager, heir number three and his agent. There were nine people present, and each one seemed to have a different perspective. I got the listing, but, now I'm a bit apprehensive about the contract negotiation process."

The agent is right to be concerned. Do you suppose those nine people have the same agenda with regard to the sale of that property? Probably not. If the listing presentation was complex, what's the contract negotiation going to be like? Probably more complex.

In a situation like this, you should go into the listing presentation with several objectives in mind. The first goal is to get the listing. The second objective is to get the group to agree to a single spokesperson. Third, get agreement on what the specific decision-making process will be for dealing with a purchase offer. You might also ask that one individual in the group be the designated decision maker. The odds of getting a single decision maker may not be high, but asking for one may help you negotiate a single spokesperson and clarify the need for a clear group decision making process. People skills and good communication will be important attributes for the listing agent in this complex situation.

Your marketing skills must be sharper, and your resources more extensive. Effectively pricing and marketing luxury homes require creativity and expertise. The luxury market is not real estate 101. You must be able to do a market analysis on a property for which comparables are scarce. You need to know how to target the most likely buyer categories for the lifestyle a home represents and know how to reach those groups with a compelling sales message. You need to know how to create a well thought out marketing plan for a specific property. You need to create marketing pieces, ads, and Web pages with strong copy and quality photography. You must network with other real estate professionals and with others who work with the affluent. Your negotiation skills must be strong. And, you must understand and meet the needs and high expectations of your wealthy clientele.

All in all, if you target the upper-tier market, you must recognize up front that you will probably have to invest more time and more marketing dollars. But, remember, the financial rewards are greater, too. Expect to be patient with luxury buyers; they often move slowly and may have to wait for just the right house (representing just the right lifestyle) to come on the market (inventory is smaller). You may also encounter additional players who add complexity to the transaction. On the other hand, if you are dealing with an all-cash transaction, you may find the contract-to-closing process is faster because financing isn't as much of an issue.

Chapter Three
Defining and Measuring the Upper-Tier Market

The definition of the upper-tier residential real estate market (what we might call the rich buyer/rich seller market) varies depending upon location.

For the purposes of this book, we can say that the upper-tier or luxury home market in any given area is the top 10 percent of residential home sales – based on price – in the last 12 months.

We use this measure at The Institute for Luxury Home Marketing and refine it further by setting a "floor" for upper-tier properties at $500,000. In other words, a property priced below $500,000, by our definition, is not a luxury home.

In some small markets, the top 10 percent of home prices might actually fall below $500,000; however, by national standards, those homes are not perceived as top-of-the market luxury homes.

Even though the luxury segment is a small percentage of homes overall, there are markets which are extremely expensive. According to Forbes magazine, in 2005 there were 123 zip codes where median or midrange home prices exceeded $1 million or more. The chart below shows the ten most expensive zip codes for 2005, seven of which were in California. The softer market which began in 2006 and 2007 may have caused these prices to slip a bit, but nonetheless, these are very pricey markets. Since this represents the market price mid-point, the top 10% in these markets will be well into the multiple millions of dollars.

Ten Most Expensive U.S. Zip Codes
(based on median housing prices)

Zip code	Community	County/State	Median Home Price
11962	Sagaponack	Suffolk, NY	$2,787,500
92067	Rancho Santa Fe	San Diego, CA	$2,445,000
92662	Newport Beach	Orange, CA	$2,397,500
94528	Diablo	Contra Costa, CA	$2,266,000
94957	Ross	Marin, CA	$2,247,500
11976	Water Mill	Suffolk, NY	$2,150,000
93108	Santa Barbara	Santa Barbara, CA	$2,050,000
90402	Santa Monica	Los Angeles, CA	$2,005,000
92661	Newport Beach	Orange, CA	$1,996,500
33190	Miami Beach	Miami-Dade, FL	$1,942,500

Source: Forbes Magazine 2006 report based on median home price by zip code for 2005

If we look at metropolitan areas, as of first quarter of 2007, we'll find seven Metropolitan Statistical Areas (MSAs) with single family median prices exceeding $500,000. This translates to half of all single family sales for the quarter exceeding $500,000. To put this in perspective, the U.S. median single family home price for first quarter of 2007 was $212,000. Median price for condos was $224,500.

Metropolitan Statistical Area	Median Single Family Sales Price 1Q 2007
San Jose-Sunnyvale-Santa Clara (CA)	$788,000
San Francisco-Oakland-Freemont (CA)	$748,100
Anaheim-Santa Ana/Orange County (CA)	$697,300
Honolulu (HI)	$620,000
San Diego-Carlsbad-San Marcus (CA)	$595,200
Los Angeles-Long Beach-Santa Ana (CA)	$589,900
NY-Wayne-White Plains (NY)	$521,400
Source: NAR, 2007	

The Size of the National Upper-Tier Home Market

Despite the fact that there are some very expensive communities, the luxury home market is a small segment of the total number of homes in the United States and luxury homes are a small proportion of the homes sold each year.

If we analyze household income, it is easy to understand why upper-tier home sales are such a small percentage of total home sales.

According to the most current U.S. Census Bureau report (as of the summer of 2007), the median income for all U.S. households is $48,200. (Remember that the median is the middle point – half the households earn more, half earn less.) So it should come as no surprise that the government views you as affluent if your total household income is as much as $100,000 annually. Households earning at least $100,000 represent about 19.0% of all of the country's estimated 116.0 million households. The top 10% of U.S. households has a median income of $184,800. The more affluent households are more likely to be homebuyers. In 2005, The National Association of Realtors® reported one in four of homebuyers claimed a household income of $100,000 or more.

In some expensive housing markets, this level of income may not be enough to guarantee you entry into the luxury home market. It is interesting to note that the median primary home value for the country's top 10% earning group was $450,000 when the Federal Reserve Board did their most recent Survey of Consumer Finances in 2004.

U.S. Household Income Estimates

Income	% of All US Households
$100,000+	19.0 %
$200,000+	3.4 %

Source: US Census Bureau 2007

The good news is that some Americans are becoming more affluent. In the past two decades, the growth in the number of households earning $100,000 (in inflation-adjusted dollars) has outpaced the total growth in households. Unless we have a dramatic decline in the economy, the fact that tens of thousands of baby boom households (those born between 1946 and 1964) are in or moving into prime earning years should create even more households with $100,000 or more in income. The small, but growing percentage of households earning at least $100,000 explains why the luxury home market is a small, but growing segment of the total.

Growth in Number of $100,000 Income Households and The Percent of Total Households They Represent

Year	Households	Number of $100,000 Households/Percent	
1980	82.4 million	4.5 million	5.5 %
1990	94.3 million	8.0 million	8.5 %
2000	106.4 million	14.2 million	13.3 %
2004	114.4 million	19.7 million	17.2 %
2006*	116.0 million	22.1 million	19.0 %

Source: U.S. Census Bureau, 2007.
*Income Households" are those households earning any income

Comparing Your Market to the Nation

Think about the top 10 percent of homes in your housing market and the income necessary to buy into that luxury home segment. Based on income, what percentage of total U.S. households would you estimate could afford to buy your latest luxury home listing? Although that's an interesting question, the more relevant question for a real estate agent working in the luxury home market is: How rich is your market?

To determine household income breakdowns in zip codes in your community, see the Community Sourcebook of ZIP Code Demographics published by ESRI Data and available in most large libraries in the business reference section. This publication contains accurate demographic information for every U.S. ZIP Code, based on the 2006/2011 projections of key population and income data.

For instance, I looked up the 75075 zip code in the fast-growing metropolitan Dallas suburban market of Plano in the Community Sourcebook of ZIP CODE Demographics. The table below will show you some of what I found.

Demographic Information for Zip Code 75075 in Plano (TX)

14,407 Households
10,282 Family Households

Percent of Households earning $100,000 – $149,999 = 24.6 %

Percent of households earning $150,000 or more = 17.2 %

Median household income = $103,456

Median age = 39.2

This zip code is one of the more affluent in the country.

For comparison, let's look at a zip code in another, even more prosperous Dallas suburb.

Demographic Information for Zip Code 75019 in Coppell (TX)

13,217 Households
10,381 Family Households

Percent of Households earning $100,000 to $149,999 = 20.3 %

Percent of Households earning $150,000 or more = 40.4 %

Median household income = $125,040

This zip code is significantly more affluent than the average U.S. zip code

Median household income for this zip code is in the top 1% of all U.S. zip codes

Even though households in both these zip codes in the same metropolitan market are more affluent than average, there is a notable difference between them in terms of earnings in the $100,000 and above range. Take the time to analyze your market area by zip code. Share the resulting data with your sellers and use it to negotiate for your buyers.

Chapter Four

Analyzing Your Local Upper-Tier Market

If you expect to be an expert in the upper-tier market, you must know and understand your market. In addition to having previewed the luxury home resale inventory and being familiar with the new home builders and their luxury home products, you must also take the time to gather and analyze the statistics relevant to the upper-tier market niche. Here are some steps to start your analysis of the market so you can position yourself as an expert and help your affluent prospects make better real estate decisions:

Define the geographic area that you serve – you personally, not your company, not your office.

Go into your multiple listing system database and identify the top 10 percent of properties sold in the last 12 months in your market area. This will define what the upper-tier is in the market area in which you work. If you prefer, you can just select whatever overall price range you wish to analyze, for instance, you might want to look at properties priced at $500,000 and above.

Take the top 10 percent of closed properties (or the overall price range you've selected) and break it into logical price bands. You decide which price ranges make the most sense for your market. A sample might look like this:

Market Price Ranges
$500,000 - $549,999
$550,000 - $599,999
$600,000 - $649,999
$650,000 - $699,999
$700,000 - $749,999
$750,000 - $999,999
$1,000,000 - $1,499,999
$1,500,000 - $1,999,999
$2,000,000 and above

In expensive markets, you might choose to start your analysis significantly higher than $500,000 and include more price bands in the multimillions.

Once you have broken your market into logical price bands, research the following for each price band:

- The percent of listings that actually sell verses those that expire

- The average days on market for each of the price bands.

- The list-to-sales-price differential (what did it list for, what did it sell for, what was the percentage of list price to sales price?)

- The approximate percentage of new homes on the market versus resale. You won't find this in MLS data; you'll have to estimate based on your market knowledge.

- The number of closed transactions in each price range or price band.

- The listing term that your competition is getting in each price range. This statistic will be your "best guess" since MLS probably doesn't record this.

You are probably thinking that you already know these statistical averages for the total listing inventory in your MLS. But the averages are irrelevant when it comes to the upper-tier market. It's important to calculate these things for each of the price bands in the top ten percent, because the statistics will be different.

Once you have this information, how are you going to use it? Let's analyze the sample market that I have broken into price bands in the list above.

Days-on-market

Here is a sample chart tracking average days on market by price range for an imaginary market. Take your market's data to create your chart.

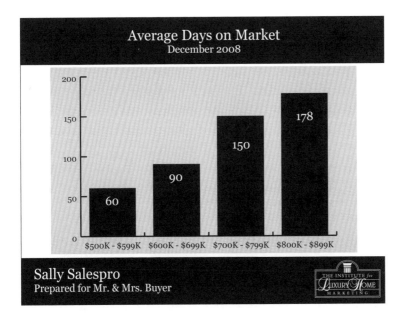

As you might have expected, the sample chart shows that it takes longer to sell the more expensive properties. How can you use the information? Assume you have someone whose property you believe should be listed just under $700,000. They, on the other hand, are convinced the home needs to be priced just above $700,000. There's a full two month's difference in selling time between the two price ranges, as based on the current market. For an expensive home, the costs associated with carrying that property for an extra two months plus the inconvenience of a slower sale can be substantial, especially if your seller is transferring or trying to time a sale with the closing on another property. This statistic gives you the information you need to negotiate price more effectively with your seller. You may already be doing this using average statistics for the overall market, but it's much more powerful if you know exactly what is happening in the market by individual price range.

This data can also help you make better decisions. If you are listing a million-dollar property under a scenario of 220 days-on-market, you want more than a six-month listing. You wouldn't be satisfied with six months because it's not giving you even the average number of days on market for a property to sell in that price range. You'll want a longer listing term in order to have a fair chance to sell the property. Given the marketing costs associated with a million-dollar-plus listing, it can be an expensive proposition if your listing term is too short and the seller doesn't relist with you. Taking the time to analyze the market gives you the information to make good business decisions such as the listing term to request.

Average days on market will tell you the minimum listing term you want based on the probable sales price. Sharing this selling time expectation with the homeowner at the listing stage will also help your seller develop realistic expectations. This also can open a dialogue about the relationship between price and selling time.

Buyers by price range

One of the most important bits of information to gather is the number of buyers by price range. On the chart below titled Number of Real Buyers by Price Range, I have simply plotted the number of homes sold and closed by price range for the most recent month in an imaginary market. The same chart in your market might look very different, but the concept is what's important, not whether this is reflective of your marketplace. Notice the terminology; the chart's title refers to the number of real buyers by price range. The number of sales (closed trans-actions) in each price range is the same as the number of real buyers who actually purchased homes in that price range and closed on them. In this business, we typically talk about the number of properties sold or the number of sales, but let me ask you a question: If you list a $750,000 house does your seller believe that there are buyers on every corner? Usually the seller overestimates the demand in the market. But if you will track this statistic and make a simple change in terminology, it may help your seller recognize that buyers for high-priced homes may not be waiting on every corner.

Talk about NUMBER OF REAL BUYERS as opposed to closed transactions or homes sold. To clarify this for your clients, define real buyers by saying, "By the way, I'm defining a real buyer as one who not only contracts for a home, they show up at closing and leave owning the house." Using "number of real buyers" instead of "number of sales" with your sellers can be a dose of reality. "In the last 30 days, in the price range where you want to list your home, there have been just six real buyers. And it has taken an average of 175 days of marketing to find each of those buyers." That's powerful information!

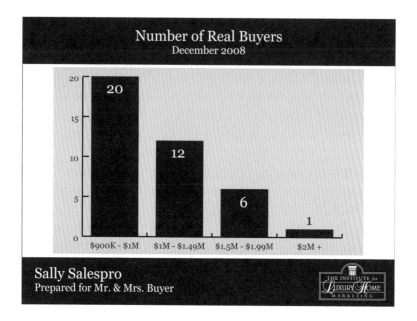

Negotiate list price using Number of Real Buyers. Let's assume you have a seller who wants to list at just over $1.5 million and you think the list price needs to be a bit under $1.5 million. You can say to that seller, "In the last six months, in the price range where you would like to list your property, there have been six real buyer per month. However, if we keep it under $1.5 million we are in a price range where there have been twelve buyers per month. We're doubling the odds of selling your home." When you can justify why you are recommending a particular list price and show the seller specific statistics regarding the alternate price ranges, you are educating your seller to the reality of the market. You are also more likely to receive a properly priced listing.

You can also use this tool when you represent the buyer. It's very effective when presenting a contract to be able to show the listing agent and/or seller that, "There were only twelve real buyers in this price range in the last month. My buyer is qualified, likes the house, and is ready to purchase. With so few buyers out there, doesn't it make sense to do this deal?"

Gather the statistics, change your terminology from "sales" to "number of real buyers," and take the time to make the charts so that you have a visual tool to use with your buyers and sellers.

Author's Note: Many members of The Institute for Luxury Home Marketing asked us to make it easy for them to create the charts and graphs talked about in this section. As a result, My Market Graphs™ software is available to Institute members in the members' only section of our Website (www.Luxury-HomeMarketing.com). You collect the data for the time period and price ranges you choose, enter it in one simple worksheet, and the software does the calculations and creates the charts and graphs. Charts are customized with your name and can be printed, added to your Website and included in your Power-Point presentations.

The odds of selling your home

As you do your upper-tier market analysis, create a chart called "The Odds of Selling Your Home." In the sample below, I've broken a real market into price bands and I've pulled the MLS data on the number of listings (on a given day) in each price range as well as the number of properties sold (real buyers) in each price range over the past 90 days. Then, I've done a simple calculation, dividing the number sold (or real buyers) by the number of listings. This is simply a look at demand relative to supply.   We can call the resulting number the odds of selling your home in that price range in the last 90 days. As you can see, the odds in the chart range from a low of zero percent to a high of 77 percent.

It's interesting to note how the odds vary. In this market, the two highest odds are not the two lowest price bands. The second most active segment in this particular market is $700,000 to $799,999. Doing this calculation identifies which price bands are the most active, and you can sit down with your sellers and talk about the actual odds of selling their home based on the current activity in their price range. Calculate this for several time periods. You might look at the last 12 months, the last quarter, and the last 30 days.

The Odds of Selling Your Home

Price	Real Buyers	# Homes For sale	Odds
500,000-599,999	138	179	77%
600,000-699,999	87	185	47%
700,000-799,999	73	132	55%
800,000-999,999	20	60	33%
1m – 1,499,999	11	44	25%
1.5 m – 1,999,999	10	40	25%
2 m -- 2,999,999	6	25	20%
3 m and up	0	12	0%

You can do this same price band comparison with pending sales, which gives you an even more current picture of the odds of selling your home. If you think your market conditions are changing, comparing sold statistics to pending statistics can be very useful.

Notice on the "Odds of Selling Your House" chart above, that while the odds of selling generally decline as price increases, there is one price band where that is not true. Look at the $700,000 - $799,999 price range. The odds of selling in this price band are actually higher than in the price range $600,000 - $699,999.   In real estate we're taught that listing lower is always better than listing higher. That's wrong. It is not always better to list a property lower. Instead it is a question of demand relative to supply. In this situation, if you were listing a custom home which could reasonably be listed just below $700,000 or just above $700,000, you'd be wise to list it above. Or, perhaps you might list right at $700,000 to catch those looking up to $700,000 as well as those starting their search there.

The sale-to-expiration ratio is also a useful statistic to track by price range. It illustrates the same trends in demand that the Odds of Selling Your Home calculations will reveal.

Where are your buyers coming from?

It is also useful to track – by price range – where your buyers are coming from. Doing this company-wide will give you valuable information that will help you market more effectively. Here's an example of how you might use the information:

An agent in Florida listed a million-dollar-plus property on a canal. On the shore of the canal was a boat slip that would accommodate a boat of up to 120 feet. Fortunately for this agent, her company tracks where their buyers come from. She knew that in the over $1 million price range, there was a 70 percent chance that her buyer would come from Florida or several other states. Given the price of the property, she assumed that the buyer prospects for the home would need to be multi-millionaires. So, she rented a mailing list of multi-millionaires who lived in Florida and those other key states. She further specified that she only wanted the names of those on the list who owned boats of at least 40 feet in length. She created a brochure with a cover letter and did a mailing to the people on that list. She had a number of inquiries, had several showings and sold the property to someone on that list. That's a very targeted, cost effective, and time efficient way to market. If you can target your buyer in this way – including geographically – the chances are good you can find a relevant mailing list. (More on this in Chapter 9.)

If your firm is not already tracking where buyers come from, you may want to suggest that it start doing so. Your firm probably has a form which must be filled out before a transaction is closed and commissions are distributed. By simply adding a line which asks where the buyer of the property came from, your firm can begin collecting this information. The zip code is what you need. Then, if someone at the company will create a data base containing property address, purchase price, and buyer's zip code, you'll be well on your way to being able to track buyers.

Author's Note: Look in the members' only section of The Institute's Website to find information about a reputable list broker who offers discounts on list rentals to our members. Numerous lists of the affluent are available through this source. You can also secure lists through other list houses or list brokers.

Monitor new home inventory

In some markets there is an opportunity to list and market new homes for builders. Even if this opportunity does not exist in your community, it is important to be familiar with the new luxury home inventory. New homes are competitive with the resale homes that you list. Buyers will compare values, so it is important that you know both the competitive resale product and the new home inventory in order to price your resale listings appropriately. You will also find that sometimes a new home will be a better comparable than a resale if the new home has features and amenities that match your subject property or was built by the same builder. Knowing the market means being knowledgeable about both new and resale homes.

Use information to position yourself as an expert

Taking the time to gather information not only makes you more knowledgeable about the market and gives you information to use to inform and negotiate with buyers and sellers but also can help you position yourself as an expert. Here's an example of how a real estate professional who attended one of our Institute training sessions told me she used her market data to capture builder business.

She went back to her town which she said was logically two distinct markets – the north side of town and the south side of town. She did a price band analysis for each part of her market, creating the charts and graphs which illustrated what was going on in the upper-tier. There was a local builder in her town whose business she had been trying to get for a very long time. So she decided that since she now had all this great new information, she would call him. So she called and said, I would like one hour of your time, and I guarantee you that this will be time well spent. The builder agreed to meet with her, she sat down with him, and went over all of the market information. At the end of that meeting the builder said to her, "You're right, this has been extremely valuable. I was getting ready to buy some land in the south part of town and build in a particular price range, but after looking at the reality of the market, I'm not going to do that. Instead, I'm going to buy some land in the northern part of town and build in a totally different price range. And, you've got the listings."

This agent established her credibility and provided market knowledge that was valuable to her builder prospect.

One of the fastest ways you can build visibility and credibility as a luxury home expert is to develop a regular Market Update Report which you send out on a regular basis to your target market. This Market Update Report should include relevant charts and graphs and other market information of interest to affluent buyers and sellers. You might include insights on luxury home design trends and reports on record-breaking sales. Mail or email this on a monthly basis and you'll soon be firmly positioned in people's minds as the agent who knows the upper-tier market.

Here's an example of a new agent who took this idea to the next level: A young man in a Detroit suburban area started in the residential real estate business right out of college with the goal of specializing in upper-tier waterfront properties. The first thing he did was gather information about the market. He pulled MLS data for the top 10 percent of the market and calculated the important statistics.

Since he was a decent writer, he took the statistical information that he had gathered and he wrote six short articles about what was happening in the upper price ranges along the lakeshore in suburban Detroit. He sent the six short articles to the business editor (not the real estate editor) of The Detroit Free Press, the major newspaper in the market.

Sure enough, he got a phone call from the editor indicating they'd never had such specific information about what was happening in the upper-tier lakefront property market. The editor asked permission to run the articles, one a week for the next six weeks on the front page of the Saturday business section. He told the agent he would be featured as a guest contributor with photograph and byline.

The agent's branch manager told me that the week the second article ran, the young agent's phone was already ringing with people saying, "I understand you're the expert in lake shore properties. We'd like to have you come out and talk about listing our home," or "I see that you're the expert in lake front properties. We're interested in buying. When can we talk about getting together?" This was a brand new agent doing a good job of creating the perception that he was an expert. He jump-started his business.

His next very important step was to demonstrate his competence. Since he was so new, he went to his manager and asked to be teamed up with an experienced agent with whom he could share this initial business and who could guide him through the transactions. He understood that he had positioned himself as the expert and now he had better be able to deliver on that promise. Working with an experienced agent allowed him to bring necessary competence to the transactions.

Chapter Five

Targeting Rich Buyer and Rich Seller Prospects

Old money, new money, and the ultra consumer

When I first started training real estate agents to work in the luxury home market, somebody said to me, "Laurie you should distinguish between the attitudes of old money and new money consumers, because there are differences." I also decided that there is an important third category, what we might call the ultra consumers or strained affluent. These are the folks who are stretching to live as affluent a lifestyle as possible. They s-t-r-e-t-c-h to live in an expensive home, to drive an expensive a car, and to dress as well as possible.

As real estate agents we love these ultra consumers because typically they are fueling the upper-tier. They come in at the entry level of the luxury home market and allow other affluent households to buy up. They also represent a large part of the luxury home market segment. If we compare them to those with new money and old money mindsets, they probably share more of the characteristic of new money prospects.

What are the old money/new money differences? The differences listed below are generalizations, but they serve the purpose of stimulating you to ask yourself some important questions about your prospects. Remember, in some cases these differences have less to do with the age of the money and more to do with attitude or mindset.

Old money may be cash poor. They simply may not have access to their funds. Their money may be tied up in trusts or controlled investments.

Old money may want you to be discreet, discreet, discreet. To illustrate, I have a friend who sells real estate in Connecticut not far from New York City. Her community is an old money market with a great many beautiful estate properties. One day she received a phone call from a homeowner who said, "I would like you to come out and talk about listing our estate. However, we want you to know up front that we have some marketing ground rules."

She said, "I'd be delighted to market your home for you. What are the ground rules?"

They said, "First ground rule, we don't want a sign."

"That's not a problem," she answered. "In fact, in this community, we're are restricted from using signs."

They continued, "We want no mention of our home in the multiple listing system. We want no advertising. We don't want anyone in your office to know it's for sale. In fact, we don't want anybody to know it's for sale. We just want you to sell it."

Now that's a bit of a challenge. Fortunately, the agent has worked in that marketplace for more than 35 years and she knows just about everybody in her community. So, she sat down and defined the kind of buyer who would enjoy the lifestyle the property represented and would be able to afford the home.

She thought about all the people she knew in her community and in her sphere of influence who matched her definition of a likely buyer, and she began to telephone them. She said, "IF I were able to bring onto the market a property which meets the following description, would you have an interest?" She also called a short list of other area real estate professionals and explained that she was working on a private, confidential sale and might they have a prospect. She sold the home as a result of one of her calls. This is an example of how old money sometimes wants you to be discreet to the point of almost tying your hands behind your back in terms of marketing. Don't be surprised if old money prospects want to protect their privacy.

Old money may also be conservative in the product they buy. Often they prefer a totally different kind of home with a different set of amenities than do new money prospects. They may gravitate to a traditional property while new money may lean toward something a bit flashier.

Old money may be less likely to look wealthy. Don't fall into the trap of evaluating people based on how they look. Not long ago, high tech markets had lots of dot-com millionaires. Agents in cities like Seattle, San Francisco, and Austin talked about "twenty-somethings" who ambled into the real estate office in shorts and flip-flops wanting to buy a house. The next thing the agents knew they were handling all cash transactions for million-dollar-plus properties. The dot-com millionaires may be less common than they were a just a few years ago, but it's still dangerous to jump to conclusions based on how prospects look. A broker in Florida is still embarrassed about instructing his assistant to tell the old guy in the overalls who came in to inquire about buying land, that the manager was out for the day. What did the "old guy" do? He drove his pickup truck to another office where an agent happily sold him the land for the first Super Wal-Mart in Florida. The less than wealthy looking client was the second richest man in America at the time – Sam Walton. Don't judge people's pocketbooks based on appearances, especially in the case of old money prospects that may not necessarily look affluent.

On the other hand, your new-money prospects are earning their money now, they have access to their funds and these new-money clients may be all cash buyers.

New money may be comfortable with publicity. If you sell the most expensive property ever sold in your market area, and you and your manager want to send out a press release announcing the record setting sale, your old money homebuyer may say, "Please don't!" and have palpitations of the heart just thinking about it. New money, on the other hand, may not only give you permission to contact the media, they may volunteer to stand in front of the house for the photograph.

New money may want a little more flash – a trophy house with impressive amenities. An agent in New England recently shared a story about new money buyers who purchased a home in a prestigious old money area. The neighborhood was so wooded, the agent told me, that you felt like you were driving down a country lane. Part of its charm and desirability was that you couldn't see the homes, just the gates and mailboxes.

"I was shocked," she said, "when I dropped by about six months after closing. The trees screening their home were gone. When I asked if the trees had caught a disease and died, they said no, they had cut them down so that everyone could see their beautiful home." Privacy was less important than visibility. Different people have different priorities.

While these points are generalizations, they should spark your thinking about your prospects and where they stand on issues such as privacy or the desire for a trophy home. These points should raise some questions to think about as you work with a new prospect. Understanding prospects' points of view and lifestyle choices can give you valuable insight into how to work with them more effectively, whether they have old or new money attitudes.

For a more sophisticated, research-based look at the differences of prospects within the wealthy market segment, read The Institute's White Paper on Lifestyle Marketing to the Six Categories of Affluent. Information on this report can be found at www. LuxuryHomeMarketing.com.

Categories of luxury home buyers and sellers

If we define the luxury market to include $500,000 and above homes, we could include the categories below in our target list of prospects for buying and selling luxury homes. We could break the luxury market into other segments as well, but these general categories offer some useful insights into the luxury home niche and highlight the fact that rich buyers and rich sellers are not all alike.

Affluent households with high incomes who often spend most of what they earn to support an affluent lifestyle. This group is often called "ultra-consumers."

Million Dollar Asset Households are closely related to the group above but have accumulated significant assets even though they may not have high net worth. They are often spenders rather than savers. We could call these folks the ultra-ultra consumers.

Atypical millionaires (the not typical millionaires) who are spending their money. Most millionaire households are savers who don't live in an upper priced property. Surprised? Read the books The Millionaire Next Door and The Millionaire Mind by Tom Stanley. While these books are several years old, the concepts are still true. The majority of wealthy individuals are self-made and came from the middle-class. They tend to bring their middle-class values with them, resulting in conservative spending patterns, at least initially.

Owners of million and multi-million dollar homes Regardless of whether these homeowners have watched appreciation take their homes into the luxury realm or purchased a pricey property to start with, at some point they made be sellers. Remember that in lower priced markets, you will need to adjust this price to be reflective of where your city's luxury home market begins.

Inheritors There is a huge transfer of wealth occurring as the Depression and World War II generations pass their assets to adult Baby Boomers. There is also the beginning of a transfer of wealth from Boomers to Generation Xers.

Wealthy immigrants and International buyers and sellers Immigrants are more likely to become millionaires than the average American. International consumers are an increasing factor in the luxury segment, especially in major markets.

The über rich These are the very wealthiest households. We'd all like to have them on our client list!

Affluent households

As reported earlier in this book, based on a August 2007 Census

Bureau report, the median household income in the U.S. is $48,200. That means half of U.S. households earn more, half earn less. Only the top 17.2% of households earn as much as $100,000. The top 3.18% earn as much as $200,000.

If the median income is lower than you might have guessed, here's an interesting statistic for comparison. The annual median income for Realtors® was $47,700, as reported by NAR in May of 2007. Break this down by license type and you find that sales agents earned a median income of $34,400 while the comparable figure for brokers was $73,700. Those Realtors® with two years or less experience in the business earned $15,300 in median income

U.S. Household Income Distribution

Income	Number of Households	Percentage
$100,000 - $149,999	11,257,636	10.66 %
$150,000 - $199,999	3,543,795	3.55 %
$200,000 or more	3,357,610	3.18 %
		17.2 %

Source: Census Bureau, Selected Income Characteristics, 2005

While the median household income in the United States is just a bit above $48,000 annually, the top quartile of families fare substantially better. Mendelsohn Media Research, based in New York City, has spent more than 25 years doing extensive research to track the spending and other habits of the top quartile of the nation's households as measured by income. The 2006 Mendelsohn Affluent Head of House Survey, HHI $85,000+ & nbsp breaks the top quartile (actually about the top 23%) of the nation's households into three income categories – $85,000 to just under $100,000, $100,000 to just under $200,000 and $200,000 and above

Mendelsosohn's income analysis is consistent with US Census

Bureau data which shows 5.8% of households earn between $85,000 and $99,999 annually while another 17.2 % earn in excess of $100,000.

Although Mendelsohn's first income category is bit below the $100,000-plus income range we are most interested in, the study's statistics and insights are interesting and relevant to any analysis of affluent consumers.

How do they make their money? The majority of heads of households earning $85,000 or more fall into the broad occupational categories as seen in the chart below.

Occupations of Affluent Heads of Households
(Employed heads of households earning $85,000 or more)

Management/Business/Finance	38%
Professional*	28%
Sales and office	17%
Service	6%
Other	11%

* Includes doctors, dentists, lawyers, and other professionals

Source: 2006 Mendelsohn Affluent HOH Survey, HHI $85,000+ & nbsp © Mendelsohn Media Research, NYC, 2006

Nationally, the affluent market is dominated by a high proportion of business owners, self-employed professionals, CEOs, and other top corporate executives. There are other important occupational segments. Some markets have affluent media personalities, entertainers, or sports figures. Other markets may have large concentrations of successful lawyers, doctors, or top sales people. Analyze the affluent occupational segments in your community and identify the opportunities. Identifying the occupations of the affluent allows you to target these households more effectively and to customize your marketing approach. (See the marketing ideas section for examples of how to do this.)

High earners are Online

Numerous research studies indicate that affluent homebuyers and sellers are using the Internet in their real estate information gathering and expect their agents to be using e-mail and promoting listings Online. (There's more on this later in the book.)

The 2006 Mendelsohn's Affluent Head of Household Survey, Household Income $85,000+ documents this. The wealthy are using the Web. Of the households earning $200,000 or more, 97% use a computer at home, 49% spend more than 11 hours Online weekly, and 88% say they communicate via e-mail. Fifty-seven percent report having three or more computers at home. The Web is a news source and financial management tool for these householders: Sixty seven percent get their news Online. Fifty-three percent use it to obtain information about financial products, 55% bank Online, and 24% actually conduct financial securities transactions on the Internet.

Although the survey did not specifically look at the use of the Internet in real estate, the National Association of Realtors' 2006 Profile of Home Buyers and Sellers indicates that 80% of homebuyers used the Internet as a resource when shopping for a home and 24% first saw the home they bought Online. Given the high use of the Internet by the affluent, it seems reasonable to assume that the use of the Internet to research properties is even greater among rich buyers and sellers. What's more, research from Dan Richard of The Gooder Group, a Virginia-based real estate marketing company, indicates that about three-fourths of those going Online to look at properties do so before contacting a real estate agent. This is changing the way prospects choose their real estate agents, making it more important than ever before that you have your listings Online and that you respond as quickly as possible (within hours, not days) to all e-mail queries from prospects. If you are not available to respond to your email, consider adding an auto responder that lets others know that their email was received and that you will be responding to their communication soon

High earners are active in sports

Heads of household earning $200,000 or more still find time to exercise and participate in sports. They are significantly more likely than the general population to go sailing, play tennis, snow ski, sail, play golf, and go power boating. The sporting activities most often pursued (based on the average number of days the affluent heads of households participated in the activity in the past 12 months) are listed below. You'll also find the affluent attending spectator sporting events.

Participation in Sports by $200,000+ Income Group

Sport	# Of days participated
Fitness Workout	82 days
Fitness Walking	70 days
Jogging	67 days
Flying a plane	48 days
Golf	29 days
Swimming	29 days

Source: 2006 Mendelsohn Affluent HOH Survey, HHI $85,000+ & nbsp © Mendelsohn Media Research, NYC, 2006

As income rises, you'll also find that attendance at the theatre, non-classical concerts, and museums goes up as well. If these are activities that you enjoy, you may find that the people you interact with while participating in sports and cultural events may also be business prospects. Remember, however, that building a relationship is an important first step.

"Million Dollar Asset" households

The three charts that follow look at households that have accumulated at least $1 million worth of major assets. These households are identified by Mendelsohn as Million Dollar Asset households to differentiate them from true millionaires, as defined by the traditional formula for millionaires -- assets minus liabilities equals net worth. We might call this group the ultra-ultra consumers. Uber consumers, if you prefer.

It is important to note that Mendelsohn's Million Dollar Asset households are NOT necessarily millionaire households, since Mendelsohn's calculation is an asset-plus-income figure as opposed to a net worth calculation. The Million Dollar Asset households have at least $1 million when you total the value of their home, any other real estate they own, the face value of insurance policies, stocks or other securities, and the amount of their annual income. Mortgages, debts, or other liabilities are not part of Mendelsohn's analysis. However, Mendelsohn's Million Dollar Asset household is a household with significant assets and an affluent lifestyle.

By contrast, in a millionaire household all the assets minus all the liabilities results in a NET figure equaling or exceeding $1 million.

The chart below takes the top quartile (actually the top 23%) of U.S. households, breaks it into three income groups, and then looks at the percentage each group represents of the total of high income households. It also takes the households in the top quartile that have at least $1 million in assets ("Million Dollar

Asset" households) and shows which income group (as a percentage) those "Million Dollar Asset" (MDA) households come from.

Analyzing the Top Quartile of U.S. Households

Income	% of the top earning quartile	% of MDA households*
$85,000 to just under $100,000	26%	22%
$100,000 to just under $200,000	61%	63%
$200,000 and above	13%	15%

*Percent of total Million Dollar Asset Households represented by each income group
Source: Census Bureau, Selected Income Characteristics, 2005

Average Value of Principal Residence

Percent of "Million Dollar Asset" household's total assets represented by principal residence

Income	Total Assets	% Home*	Home Value
$85,000 to just under $100,000	$922,300	35%	$322,800
$100,000 to just under $200,000	$1,286,600	32%	$411,700
$200,000 and above	$3,058,200	22%	$672,800

*This figure is the percentage home value represents of total assets
Source: 2006 Mendelsohn Affluent HOH Survey, HHI $85,000+ & nbsp © Mendelsohn Media Research, NYC, 2006

While many of these Million Dollar Asset households may also have mortgages, car loans, credit card debt, and other liabilities that keep them from the ranks of true millionaires, they are affluent spenders, they populate the lower level of upper-tier home buyers and sellers, and there are lots of them. By and large, this is an excellent prospect group for luxury homes. Remember that the home values above are averages, so many in this Million Dollar Asset household group buy expensive homes.

Millionaires

Millionaire households are those whose net worth (or total assets minus liabilities) equals $1 million or more. For comparison, according to a recent Federal Reserve report, the median household net worth in the U.S. is about $93,000.

TNS, one of the world's largest market information companies conducts an annual Affluent Market Research Program (AMRP) which estimates the number of millionaires Their formula for millionaires is assets - liabilities = net worth, however; they exclude the primary residence and any debt against it from the equation. Among the key survey findings (as of mid-2006) were the following, quoted from their press release:

The number of U.S. millionaire households has risen to a record high of 9.3 million as of mid-2006. This is an increase of five percent from the prior year, and the fourth consecutive year that the population of millionaires has increased. (For this study, millionaires are defined as having $1 million in net worth excluding primary residence.)

Growth in Number of Millionaire Households (2001 To 2006)

Year	Number Millionaire HHs (In millions)	% Increase over prior year
2006	9.3	5 %
2005	8.9	9 %
2004	8.2	33 %
2003	6.2	13 %
2002	5.5	-9 %
2001	6.0	-4 %

Source: TNS Financial Services, 2006

Author's Note: About the TNS Financial Services Affluent Market Research Program: AMRP has been providing the financial services community with critical data and insights since 1981. The study is based on a representative national sample of over 1,600 households with a net worth of $500,000 or more, excluding primary residence.

The chart below identifies some of the places where millionaires congregate – the 10 counties with the most millionaires.

**Top Ten U.S. Counties
With Highest Number of Millionaire Residents**

Rank

Rank	County	
1	Los Angeles County, CA	268,136
2	Cook County, IL	171,118
3	Orange County, CA	116,157
4	Maricopa County, AZ	113,414
5	San Diego County, CA	102,138
6	Harris County, TX	99,504
7	Nassau County, NY	79,704
8	Santa Clara County, CA	74,824
9	Palm Beach County, FL	71,221
10	King County, WA	68,390

Source: TNS Financial Services, 2006

Despite the frequent perception that the average millionaire is a high roller, the average millionaire might be characterized by three words – frugal, frugal, frugal. You are more likely to find the typical millionaire shopping at Costco and Target than Saks or Neiman Marcus (although they most likely shop in those stores as well). But in general, research says the average millionaire achieved his or her financial status by saving, not spending.

This frugal spending pattern translates to their homes as well. Millionaire residences are very often not in the top 10% of a market's homes. However, even conservative savers may decide to move up when certain lifestyle changes occur. Retirement or the sale of a business will often trigger a luxury home purchase ("We've worked hard, we deserve it!"). Sometimes a divorce will result in at least one luxury purchase. This makes it important to network with those who may be aware when these changes are occurring – from business brokers to CPAs and attorneys.

I recently encountered an example of the frugal millionaire attitude in Las Vegas where I was speaking at a national convention. I asked a bellman, a young man in his early thirties, to help me move several boxes of materials into the meeting room. When he realized that the meeting was a national real estate convention, he started talking to me about his financial theories.

"You know," he said, "My wife and I bought a nice house here in Vegas with eighteen hundred square feet and a pool. We have just one child so we have plenty of room. We're making mortgage payments twice a month so we can pay off our mortgage faster. In seven more years my mortgage will be fully paid.

"I'm also a saver," he said. "I have an I.R.A and an annuity stock investment program. It's my goal to retire by age 50, move back home to Florida, buy a new house and a boat, and do nothing but play golf. My wife is saying we need to buy up and I'm saying, no honey, we need to retire at age fifty."

This young man may not be a millionaire, at least not YET. But his philosophy is consistent with the mentality that creates millionaires. Research profiles the average millionaire as someone who consistently saves 15 to 20 percent of his or her gross annual income and spends conservatively.

Oops! The average millionaire doesn't look like the best prospect for upper-tier properties. **It is the atypical (or NOT typical) millionaire we want, the one who has made money and is now spending it**. Two quick suggestions for spotting these individuals include: watching the lists of insider/executive stock sales for publicly held companies in your market (you can find these reports Online), and networking with business brokers to find successful business owners who are selling their firms and will have the proceeds to make lifestyle changes. If you can develop or purchase lists of millionaires, do market to individuals on those lists. At some point, the frugal millionaire may decide to enjoy a life style change and spend his children's inheritance.

Owners of million and multi-million dollar homes

What's the profile of these rich homeowners? While some owners of luxury homes have purchased properties and subsequently seen them appreciate to luxury price levels, many have bought expensive properties. Insights about those who can afford to buy expensive homes can be helpful in your marketing. NAR and Unique Homes magazine have conducted joint research on buyers of million-dollar homes. The sample focused on those who had purchased their home within two years of the survey. In general, this group is younger, has a smaller family, and earns substantially more than the average millionaire. Here are some of the key findings:

Million-Dollar Buyer profile
- 47 years old
- Married with one child
- 86% purchased through a real estate agent
- 54% used a luxury home magazine as an information source
- 20% bought more than 500 miles away from previous residence
- They take their time when shopping for a home! Forty percent looked for six months or more, 28% looked for a year.

The million dollar home prospect is more likely to use a real estate agent than the average buyer or seller. More than half of them used a luxury home magazine as a resource when looking for property. This use of magazines is important to know when you are creating your marketing plan for a million-dollar-plus listing. The fact that two out of 10 buy more than 500 miles away from their previous home emphasizes the importance of doing regional and national promotion (putting your listings on the Internet is important in this price range). Million-dollar home-buyers will also require your patience since they take their time when shopping for a home which best matches their lifestyle.

Multi-Million Dollar Home Owner Profile

The Institute for Luxury Home Marketing and Unique Homes magazine combined forces to research owners of multi-million dollar homes. Here's a bullet point summary of what we discovered:

Profile of affluent homeowners

- Most are married 89%

- Nearly three out of four are age 55 or younger 73%

- Most made their own fortunes

- Only 6% inherited 20% or more of their net worth

- Most were born in the U.S. 86%

- A few own residences abroad 8%

- Most are top corporate executives, self-employed professionals or business owners 81%

What the affluent spend money on
When asked their attitude about the statement, "I like living in a way which calls attention to me," the majority disagree.

However, the majority agree with the statement, "I deserve the luxuries I enjoy, I've earned them." They report the following spending:

- Home electronics exceeding $1000 84%
- Gourmet restaurant dining 83%
- Fine art, oriental carpets or antiques exceeding $1000 81%
- A jewelry item priced above $1000 68%
- Vacation travel abroad 65%
- A child or grandchild's private school tuition 62%
- Wine or champagne by the case 54%
- A car priced above $50,000 49%
- Garden tools or accessories exceeding $1000 46%

What their homes are like

- The majority live in a single family home 89%
- More than four bedrooms 78%
- A home office 84%
- More than four bathrooms 92%
- Broadband Internet connections 62%
- Wireless home network 46%
- Internet connections 95%
- Home theater 34%
- Separate guest houses 19%
- Staff quarters 19%

Location, Location, Location

- Waterfront or water view 58%
- Gated community 18%

- Golf course property 5%
- Suburban 39%
- Downtown 8%
- Outside the U.S. 8%

When buying property

- 70% own more than one personal residence
- 50% indicated that their most recently purchased residence was 500 miles or more from their closest other residence
- 27% own three or more homes
- 36% own other residential real estate as investments
- 97% used a real estate agent
- 57% very satisfied with their agent
- 54% very likely use the agent again
- 17% very unsatisfied with their agent
- 14% changed agents during the property search
- 65% closed on the home within six months of beginning the search
- 19% took more than a year
- 89% purchased a single-family residence

What they want in a real estate agent

In descending order, based on the percentage of respondents ranking the trait as "very important" in their decision-making process, here are a few of the agent characteristics ranked as important:

- Expertise in the luxury home market 70%
- Knowledge about home buying and selling process 67%
- Previous experience working with the agent 46%

- Resale home product knowledge 39%
- Ability to be discreet 36%
- Has a designation indicating experience and knowledge in the luxury home market 34%

What they want in a marketing plan
- Listing in the multiple listing service 89%
- Full-color property brochure 86%
- A special open house for agents who work the luxury home market 81%
- Open house marketing event for a carefully selected target group of prospects 44%
- Ads in luxury home magazines and Internet listings with multiple images both 53%

It is interesting to note that 42% of home buyers ranked listings with photos as important home-finding resources while 36% ranked listings with virtual tours as important.

Inheritors

The United States is in the midst of a huge transfer of wealth largely driven by the fact that the generation born in the first part of the 1900s is dying and the Baby Boom generation is inheriting. A Merrill Lynch report on the transfer of wealth, predicted this giant shift of funds. From 1996 to 2005, Merrill expected 100,000 settlements of $1,000,000 or more and an additional two million people pocketing an average of $189,000 each. This wealth transfer has helped drive real estate activity. Today's predictions are that this huge asset shift will continue to the tune of more than $41 trillion over the next few decades. While not all heirs will be made wealthy, many of them will take their new money and combine it with home equity or other assets and move up. Others will fund children's educations, buy second homes, invest in stocks and bonds, or acquire other assets.

To identify these inheritors, develop referral relationships with trust attorneys, accountants, those who probate wills, and financial advisors.

Wealthy immigrants

Wealthy immigrants are a less obvious segment to target. Immigration accounts for more than half of the population growth in the United States. Legal immigrants have been flowing into the U.S. at a rate of almost a million per year for more than two decades. Estimates are that another 300,000 come in illegally each year and remain. Immigrant households represent a high percentage of today's homebuyers and expectations are that they will represent as many as one in three of all homebuyers by 2010.

The good news for the real estate community is that although the million or so annual foreign-born arrivals to the U.S. used to move predictably to states like California, New York, Florida, and Texas, new immigration patterns began to emerge in the late 1990s. While the sheer number of new arrivals is still high in the traditional immigrant destination states, the immigrant population is growing at a faster rate in a variety of other states spread across the country from Oregon to Virginia and Idaho.

The shift in the settlement pattern of new arrivals means that immigration now helps fuel many more housing markets across the U.S. For example, Hispanics and Asians are arriving in Colorado in record numbers, Asians are moving to Nebraska, and immigrants from the former Soviet Union are flowing into Texas.

These new Americans generally share the American Dream — homeownership is an important goal and many foreign-born households reach a high homeownership rate in fewer than 10 years. Many are in a position to buy even sooner. For instance, the typical Asian immigrant comes to the U.S. with more education, a larger family, and a higher income than the average American. The Mortgage Bankers Association of America estimates that immigrants already in the U.S. could create the demand for four million or more homes over the next decade or two.

Although special government programs are available to make homeownership more easily achievable for all immigrants, the groups we are interested in are those who arrive with wealth or who accumulate wealth once they are here. In fact, households of immigrants are more likely to become millionaire households than households headed by individuals born in the U.S.

The challenge for real estate brokers and agents is to tap into this large and growing segment of the market. Language and cultural differences require that real estate professionals have new resources and competencies. Many brokerage firms publish lists of agents who speak foreign languages and promote those agents Online. Brokers are beginning to recruit more aggressively from their areas' foreign-born populations. Some agents are choosing to mentor and then partner with new agents from these cultural groups. Agents are attending special training sessions focused on building cross-cultural skills. If you are targeting this growing market segment, it will help to understand the culture, attitudes, and manners of the group you've targeted. If you aren't bilingual, find a translator who also has good people skills to assist you. Build your reputation within these groups and loyalty and referrals will often follow.

One challenge with recent arrivals can be the lack of credit ratings or financial relationships. Even their assets can be an issue. What do you do with a buyer who wants to make a down payment on a home and has jewelry and gold coins rather than a checking account?

If you want to work with affluent immigrants, you should investigate the National Association of Realtor's Certified International Property Specialist designation (CIPS). The skill-based training associated with the CIPS designation will not only help you target the international market, it will give you important insights into helping the wealthy immigrant home buyer and seller in the U.S.

The international market

Consider targeting the International market segment as part of your business strategy. The luxury and International niches are closely linked. Buyers for luxury properties in the U.S. may come from abroad and wealthy U.S. households may wish to purchase properties in other countries. In either case, you can choose to help them.

U.S. real estate has great appeal for many foreign buyers. Our country is not only viewed as being politically and economically stable, our residential prices are relatively low compared to many other locations – especially when currency valuation differences are considered. In fact, only one U.S. city makes the list of the world's top 10 cities based on most expensive home prices. London is number one with Monaco, New York, Hong Kong, Tokyo, Cannes, St Tropez, Sydney, Paris and Rome rounding out the list of pricey places as defined by "The Wealth Report" released in 2007 by real estate agency Knight Frank and Citi Private Bank.

Add safety and quality of life factors and you have a list of reasons why someone outside the country might want to buy here.

One of the markets attracting international buyers has been Florida, where buyers from other countries have recently represented 15% of ALL home buyers. Within the state, Miami has been a particular hotspot with 30.4% of buyers coming from outside the U.S. It's also interesting to note that in Florida, the foreign buyer is spending an average 17% more than the domestic buyer. Even if your marketplace has significantly fewer foreign buyers, you may want to work to capture the ones it does attract.

One could easily fill a book with the "whys and hows" of working successfully in the international market. With the single goal of helping you get started in this interesting and challenging market segment, what follows are some very important resource suggestions.

Step one is to define the International market resources Start by becoming familiar with the many international market resources NAR makes available to you as a Realtor®. NAR has identified the International market as one of their Business Specialty areas and there's no better place to start gathering information than www.Realtor.org/international/index.html. Visit the site and you'll find a wealth of information and links.

Here are a few of NAR's special offerings to help you maximize success in your international efforts:

NAR's Certified International Property Specialist designation (CIPS) training is designed to help you deal with the special challenges presented by international clients and their transactions. Sessions cover principles of international real estate – from foreign real estate business environments, capital flows and currencies to government regulations and cultures. Practical aspects of international brokerage, networking, marketing and selling are also covered.

NAR is one of about two dozen national and regional real estate associations which have formed *The International Consortium of Real Estate Associations* (ICREA). Part of ICREA's mission is to help develop international business standards, help brokers do business effectively and profitably in a growing international marketplace, and create an international referral system. As a Realtor, you can take advantage of many ICREA services.

ICREA manages **WorldProperties.com**, offering you (as a NAR member) the ability to promote your specialty and luxury properties to a targeted audience, at no cost. Properties best suited for this service include vacation and resort properties and luxury residential. If you wish to have your residential property ads displayed through WorldProperties.com's Distinctive Properties Advertising Service, you must have the listings on Realtor. com, and must be a subscriber to Realtor.com's "enhanced listing service."

This is a valuable service since it gives your luxury properties strong international visibility. Contact a Realtor.com account representative who can help you identify which of your listings would benefit from being "Internationally Featured" at Realtor.com and visible on WorldProperties.com (when the search criteria match the listing). ICREA sets no limitations on how many listings you may feature. At the time this book is being written, Realtors® can post distinctive listings on World Properties.com at no additional charge if you are a subscriber to the "enhanced listing service."

ICREA's Transnational Referral System provides a standardized referral agreement and a dispute resolution service for international referrals, all facilitated electronically. WorldProperties.com's members-only site allows access to a database of ICREA-affiliated brokers and agents.

ICREA's referral training is available in five languages and in Online and classroom formats. Successful completion of the program results in being Transnational Referral Certified (TRC).

The Global New Homes Resort portal contains a diverse portfolio of high quality new developments offered by builders worldwide. The portal allows anyone to search featured properties and view detailed information about a property, its amenities and the surrounding community. The portal allows ICREA brokers to earn fees by introducing developers to the site, serving as the listing broker for a specific project, and/or by registering clients seeking a second/holiday home for personal or investment use. All projects are broker-listed.

NAR also offers:

The Power Tools for International Practitioners Blog which is an Online resource with a wide range of timely global marketing information. Access it through the NAR Library at Realtor.org.

The Archive of Global Perspectives Quarterly Newsletter lets you search articles on a wide range of international topics.

The Monthly International eReport (Electronic Newsletter)

is available free to any NAR member. Sign up under "My Account" link on home page at www.realtor.org.

Pre-packaged Presentations – Although these are designed as sales meeting presentations, these short training modules are great self-study courses. You'll find brief information on currency and metric conversions, language issues, international tax ID numbers, Asian and Mexican business practices, and more.

Meeting, events and opportunities for international networking. Watch the Website for information on a wide range of networking events, and international meetings.

The International Real Estate Federation (FIABCI) is a 50+ year old organization based in France with offices in The U.S. FIABCI offers collaboration and networking opportunities to real estate professionals in 57 countries. Members include brokers, as well as other industry professionals. FIABCI-USA is located in Arlington (VA).

Trade Missions and Real Estate Expos are other activities which can provide networking opportunities internationally.

Start by familiarizing yourself with some of the key tools available. Then begin networking with other international agents and those who facilitate real estate transactions in the countries you wish to target.

The rich

The rich in the U.S. are getting richer. The growth in $100,000 earning households is just part of the story. The real expansion of wealth is occurring in the pockets of an even wealthier group. According to a July 2006 article in the New York Times by

Teresa Tritch; Thomas Piketty, of the École Normale Supérieure in Paris, and Emmanuel Saez of the University of California at Berkeley recently updated a groundbreaking study on income distribution in the U.S. Tritch writes, "The new figures show that from 2003 to 2004, the latest year for which there is data, the richest Americans pulled far ahead of everyone else. In the space of that one year, real average income for the top one percent of households - those making more than $315,000 in 2004 - grew by nearly 17 percent. For the remaining 99 percent, the average gain was less than three percent, and that probably makes things look better than they really are, since other data, most notably from the Census Bureau, indicate that the average is bolstered by large gains among the top 20 percent of households. In all, the top one percent of households enjoyed 36 percent of all income gains in 2004, on top of an already stunning 30 percent in 2003." In short, the rich are getting richer!

U.S. Family Earnings*

% of Families**	Income threshold***	Average Income****	Number of families
Top 10%	$92,315	$106,037	7,199,100
Top 5%	$123,408	$164,528	5,759,280
Top 1%	$276,945	$326,720	719,910
Top .5%	$407,591	$622,949	575,928
Top .1%	$1,128,525	$2,015,910	129,584
Top .01%	$5,019,015	$12,775,016	14,398

*Source: IRS data, 2004. Compilation and analysis by Piketty & Saez (2006)
http://emlab.berkley.edu/users/saez/piketty-saezOUP04US.pdf
**Relative to all families in U.S. tax paying population
***The minimum income required to fall into this group
****The average income within this group

The world's High Net Worth Individuals (HNWI) are getting richer, too. The number of rich in the world is not only increasing, the rich are getting richer. Additional good news is that in 2006, the wealthy shifted a substantially higher percentage of their investment portfolios into real estate.

According to the 2007 World Wealth Report, an annual study prepared by Merrill Lynch and CapGemini, the number of financial millionaires jumped to 9.5 million worldwide. That's up 8.3% over last year. Of the total, 3.2 million are in North America.

The report defines financial millionaires – also referred to as high net worth individuals (HNWI) -- as those with a million dollars or more in investable assets, not including their primary residences. Total wealth of the group reached $37.2 trillion in US dollars.

Last year, the global wealthy pulled substantial dollars out of "alternative investments" such as hedge funds, commodities, foreign currencies and venture capital funds. Instead, they placed a whopping 24% of their total investments into direct and indirect real estate, an increase of 50% over 2005.

While 51% of the HNWI's overall real estate investments were in commercial real estate and real estate investment trusts, a whopping 49% of the total real estate investment went into vacation and second home properties, generally not financed with mortgages. Statistics for North American millionaires are similar, with 41% of real estate investments in residential properties.

The wealthy are buying multiple homes, North American vacation and second home sales are out performing the market overall and the number of trophy properties offered in the double and triple digit millions continues to grow both in the US and abroad.

The record sale of a 20,000 square foot London penthouse over-looking Hyde Park for about $200 million to Sheikh Hamad of Qatar and the sale of a "tear down" in New York's Hamptons for $103 million, both in the first half of 2007, are evidence that the super rich see trophy homes as smart investments that also make a statement and enhance one's lifestyle.

Growing wealth is a global phenomenon. The wealthy are citizens of the world, and the demand for über homes from Dubai to London and from Moscow to New York is strong. The part of the market where luxury, vacation/second, and international homes come together is a growing segment of the market as this book goes to press.

The Über Rich: Billionaires certainly fit into the super-rich category, although the new term for those at the wealth pinnacle is the über rich! Forbes publishes a list of the world's billionaires each year. In the 2007 report, William H. Gates, III held the top spot as the world's richest man with $56 billion. Warren Buffet was right behind as second wealthiest with $52. There were 946 billionaires in the world and more than 400 of those billionaires were in the U.S. Twenty-three Canadians made the list of Billionaires in 2007, with David Thomson topping the Canadian list with $20 billion in net worth.

For more information on Forbes Billionaires, go to www.Forbes.com and click on Lists. Forbes also produces a list of the Top Earning CEOs.

Chapter Six

Understanding Motivations of Rich Buyers and Rich Sellers

The rich are different

F. Scott Fitzgerald once said to Hemingway, "The rich are different from you and me." Hemingway's less-than-star struck response was "Yes, they have more money." But they're different in some other meaningful ways. Let's look at their motivations. They are not need-oriented. They are not buying a house to have a roof over their heads. They are interested in the ideal location, architectural excellence, quality of construction, status, the view, the neighbors, and the right package of home amenities. In short, they are looking for something special, and sometimes they approach the home buying and selling process very differently from the average client. Remember, with this group you are not selling eight bedrooms and 12 baths, you are selling lifestyle.

The wealthy can afford to be spontaneous. I was talking to a California agent who said, "Let me give you an example of spontaneous. I was working with a high-powered dual career couple who called from the east coast to introduce themselves and say they were coming to California. First thing they said to me on the phone was, 'We are so excited. All of our married life, our dream has been to live in southern California on a cliff overlooking the Pacific. We cannot wait to move. We need your help in finding just the right lot, just the right builder. We are ready to build our dream home.'"

"I said, 'No problem, I can help you with that.' They came, I helped them. Eighteen months later it was time for the property to close. I sat down with them as they were finalizing the paperwork and said, 'Well what's the plan, when will the moving trucks arrive?'

"The husband said, 'Well, we need to talk to you about that. When we finish here we'd like to sit down with you and list this house.'

"After this couple had gone through eighteen months of building their dream home together what do you think my first thought was?

"List this home with me? Yes!"

"My second thought was that they were getting a divorce, that the marriage had not survived 18 months of building a home together. So, I somewhat tentatively said, 'I'll be delighted to list the house for you, but why have you decided to sell?' As you can imagine, I was expecting them to say they were divorcing.

"Instead they said, 'After going through the eighteen month process of building this house, now we know what we really want in our dream home. This house was a great dry run. We want you to find another wonderful lot with a great view for us. We love our builder, we'll stick with him, but now we are ready to build our dream property. We're going to sell this one.' This is certainly more spontaneous than the typical prospect can afford to be."

Upper-tier buyers and sellers can afford to be fickle. An agent who works in the Atlanta market was called to list a well-known estate in Buckhead, a prestigious and expensive part of town. This was a very high profile property owned by an international couple. The agent made the appointment and toured the home. She felt the house was in excellent condition. Every blade of grass in the yard looked hand trimmed. This house needed nothing. Right off the bat the seller said, "We want to sell this house as is."

The agent said, "This house certainly needs no cosmetic work."

The seller said, "No, no, you don't understand, we want to sell as is – with the Oriental rugs and the antiques in the rooms, the art on the walls, the pots and pans in the kitchen. We just want to take some of our personal possessions and leave."

If you're selling a resort condo or a wealthy individual's third or fourth home, it may not be too unusual to sell it fully furnished. In the middle of Buckhead in Atlanta, it is unusual. In old money Buckhead, chances are the buyers are going to have their own things. This situation requires a fairly complex market analysis because you're going to have to call in experts to price things other than the property. And if the buyer doesn't want all the furnishings and other contents of the home, then you may have to help coordinate the auctioning or other disposal of the contents. A fickle seller or buyer can create complexity.

Despite the story above, and to further illustrate the fickleness of the wealthy buyer, it has not been uncommon in cities with dot-com millionaires for young buyers who are busy, or perhaps not yet confident about their taste, to want to buy a fully furnished home. One good example of this occurred in Newport Coast

(CA). Pacific Design Estates, a high-end builder, created a 7,500 square foot Mediterranean design home with all the modern features and the ambiance of a Venetian palazzo. The home sold fully furnished for $8.8 million cash in five days.

Wealthy sellers and buyers can be on a different time schedule than your average buyer or seller. I was visiting an Arizona health spa one January and got up one morning to do an early morning walk through the desert. The path would accommodate two people side by side. There were probably thirty people doing this walk and everybody was bunched together in pairs. There were two ladies side by side in front of me talking about real estate. It was an interesting conversation and apparently I have no shame, because I paced myself and listened. The conversation went something like this. One was saying to the other, "We've decided to sell the estate on Long Island and my real estate agent is pushing me to put it on the market now, in January. I really think I'd prefer to list in the spring when the gardens look fabulous, but my agent keeps harping on listing it as soon as possible in January."

The seller's idea to wait might have struck me as reasonable had I not just had a conversation with a broker from Long Island. I had asked, "How's business?"

He answered, "Business is wonderful."

"In January?" I questioned. His answer wasn't what I had expected.

He said, "Laurie, in the upper tier on Long Island in the markets that I serve, January is the hottest month of the year. Don't you know what happens the end of December and first part of January in New York City?"

I shook my head no.

"The Wall Street bonuses are paid. The Wall Streeters are flush with cash and many want to move up. Long Island is an easy commute to the tip of Manhattan and we have wonderful estate properties. Thanks to Wall Street, January is my office's busiest month in the higher price ranges."

January is not the busiest month in other prices ranges on Long Island. The upper tier is on a different schedule from the rest of the market. Be sure that you are aware of anything that might create different peak periods for the high price ranges in your area.

Here are some general insights to keep in mind when working with the wealthy:

- **The rich choose what they buy based on perceived quality as well as on taste and aesthetic.** They may fall in love with the look and feel of a home, but you should take the time to talk about the quality, craftsmanship and brands they can trust. These things are important to them. But be careful not to imply they can't recognize quality and don't tell them what they need.

- **When buying, they "play to not lose" by shopping for value.** This value driven focus may explain why the number one seller of Dom Perignon champagne, the number one buyer of cashmere, and the company which sold 90,000 carats of diamonds in 2005 is Costco. Value will also be a factor in their home purchase decision. Expect them to have done pricing research Online. Be prepared to justify price with a thorough statistical analysis of the market.

- **Event marketing works in reaching the rich.** Success can breed loneliness and special events may be viewed as helping them connect with other successful people. They often want to learn to be connoisseurs, so look for creative ideas for events that are fun, exclusive and educational. Look for others who market to the wealthy and create joint events.

- **The wealthy spend an average of more than 13 hours per week Online.** Chances are good they will "research" you Online before choosing to work with you and they'll want to know they can communicate with you via email. They want complete property information Online so they can find everything they want to know about a house from their hotel room in Tokyo or their condo in Dubai at 2:00 in the morning (in their pajamas).

- **The most important characteristic they want in a salesperson is competency.** They also want to work with someone who is authentic and "puts them at ease." To succeed in this niche you must know your market and polish your skills, including your ability to establish rapport and convey your integrity. If you can establish that you share some values with them, they may feel more comfortable about working with you.

- **They have some terminology preferences.** Rather than referring to them as rich or wealthy, use the word successful. Advice culled from interviews with the wealthy says, when selling, "don't use flowery adjectives."

- **They buy stories.** While they don't like adjectives, they do like stories. Dig for the true stories that will romance your listings. The appeal of stories is part of a search for "magic" and self-identity which super successful consumers undertake.

- **They are increasingly global in their tastes, attitudes, and interests.** They often have homes in multiple countries;

their children may live abroad and most travel. As a result, their lifestyles have an international flavor.

While working with flamboyant big spenders can be fun and profitable, don't confuse them with the typical multi-million-aires who may be better characterized by Warren Buffet than P. Diddy. A high percentage of super rich are conservative, looking for quality and value, and want a real estate professional who is above all, competent, authentic and ethical.

How the rich choose real estate professionals

NAR/Unique Homes magazine research reveals these insights about rich buyers and sellers at the million dollar level and their criteria for selecting an agent:

- The affluent want an agent who knows the market (This can be further defined as knowing both the luxury market niche and the geographic market area)
- If they've used an agent before and have been happy with the agent's service, they are inclined to consider using the agent again
- The quality of the listing presentation is very important –a better listing presentation can override a previous relationship
- Affluent prospects say that offering a special luxury home marketing system will give you a marketing edge, especially if it includes a strong print advertising plan and good Internet exposure. Examples of luxury home marketing systems would include Coldwell Banker Previews,™ The RE/MAX Collection,™ Century 21 Fine Homes and Estates,™ GMAC Elegant Homes,™ ERA International Properties,™ and

Keller Williams Luxury Homes™. Marketing assistance is also offered through special organizations including Christies and Who's Who in Luxury Home Marketing. Some local and regional brokerages have their own luxury home marketing programs. If your firm doesn't have a marketing system, develop your own special program for expensive properties.

The Institute's research with Unique Homes found that multi-million dollar homeowners have similar criteria for choosing their real estate professionals. Competency is of prime importance.

Many affluent sellers are business owners, self-employed professionals, and corporate executives. These are bottom-line oriented individuals who will evaluate you based on how they perceive your ability to get the job done. In short, you must convince them that you have the skills necessary to sell the house in the time period they require, for the best price, with the least inconvenience to them.

Do you have to live the affluent lifestyle to capture upper-end business? No. But you do have to create visibility in the niche you are targeting with a focus on positioning and promoting yourself as a luxury home expert. Then, you must deliver on that promise and provide expert service.

Chapter Seven
Evaluating your competition

Analyze your competition

To determine with whom you are competing in the luxury home market, pull sales and listings in the top price ranges and look to see which brokerage firms and agents are most active. This will give you a clear picture of who is targeting this market and the market share controlled by each competitor.

Just identifying the competition isn't enough. It is also important to have a sense of what your competition is offering. Do they have a special program for luxury homes? Do they create full color brochures? Produce a special luxury magazine? Do they have a national network to use as a resource? Try to determine their strengths and weaknesses—then you can determine how best to compete. This process will also help you determine with whom you need to be networking.

The competitive analysis form below is an organized way to evaluate other brokers who compete in the upper-tier. You will be competing for prospects with these firms and their agents, so it is important to know their strengths and weaknesses. If you are a manager or broker/owner, it is especially important to do a competitive analysis of other firms targeting the upper-tier.

Competitor			Affiliation	

Profile:

# Agents		Transactions	Top 10% of Market	% Share	Top 10% of Market
# Offices		$ Volume		Up/Down?	

Agent Profile:

Three words which describe company:

	STRENGTHS	WEAKNESSES
COMPETITIVE ANALYSIS		

Strategy that they appear to be implementing?

Other comments:

In doing your analysis, look at the number of transaction sides (listings or sales) and the total dollar volume of business your competitor did in the last 12 months in the top 10 percent of the market. Calculate what percentage of the upper-tier this represents. That percentage will be their market share in the upper-tier. Is this market share trending up or decreasing? What do you perceive to be the strengths of their marketing efforts for luxury homes? Where might they be weak and vulnerable? A close review of the form will give you additional insight into analyzing the competition so you can structure your efforts to out-think and out-market them.

Chapter Eight
Recognizing the Characteristics for Success

Understanding that YOU are your product

You are in the business of listing and selling real estate, but before you can sell a home to a buyer, you must first convince the buyer that you are the agent who can best help with his or her home finding. You must sell yourself, your capabilities, your experience, and your skills. Before you can market and sell a listing, you must convince the seller that you are the agent who can best market the property. Again, you must sell yourself. In real estate, the first sale you must make is YOU. Thus, it follows that you are your product and that **you need to package, position, and promote yourself just like a product** in order to be successful in the residential real estate business.

Packaging yourself includes projecting professionalism with the way you dress. It means having a firm handshake, looking people in the eye, and carrying yourself with confidence. This sounds pretty basic, but when you are working with the affluent, most of whom are successful business people, you must be able to immediately create a favorable impression.

Positioning yourself is also important to your success. The positioning or perception that you want to create in peoples' minds is that you as a real estate sales associate are unique and better able to meet the needs of the affluent buyer and seller.

Simply stated, that should be the goal of your marketing. Then, you must deliver on that promise. You must, in fact, be unique and better able to meet their needs.

Promoting can be defined as your marketing -- how you create and communicate the perception of uniqueness for yourself and how you advertise and market your services and your listings (more on this in subsequent chapters).

Characteristics for success in the luxury niche

When I first began working in the luxury home market, I went to my broker and asked what advice she could give me about working in the luxury niche. She told me that the process of buying and selling expensive homes doesn't really differ much from the average transaction. What is different, she told me, is that the luxury home niche is a more sophisticated market and it demands a higher level of communication and professionalism—and some special characteristics. Here are the five characteristics she suggested I'd need to succeed, plus two others.

Look and act successful. In Dallas, where I live, there is a well-known broker who had a boutique luxury home company (she has since sold it). When she trained her new agents she'd tell them "fake it until you make it." Initially that made me a little bit uncomfortable. Then I realized what she was really saying. From your first day in the luxury market, you must project confidence and competence. I think she's right. One characteristic you must have is the ability to project confidence and competence.

Demonstrate professionalism and competence. The, second characteristic is to deliver on that implicit promise of by demonstrating your professionalism and competence. Projecting the right image is important, but you must also have the necessary skills.

Be unintimidated by money, power, and fame. Success characteristic number three is to be unintimidated by money, power or fame (or at least not so intimidated that you can't function). Working in the high price ranges often puts you in touch with celebrities, well-known business executives, sports stars, the fabulously rich, and other people who are high profile. An agent who is overawed or intimidated is not going to perform at peak levels.

Be memorable -- do business with style (But you don't have to live a wealthy lifestyle). You will also benefit from doing business with a little bit of style or flair. Standing out from the crowd in a positive way is good marketing. Create something that makes you memorable in the marketplace. The best way to be memorable is with service that is creative and exceptional. Clever marketing can also make you memorable. Just be sure it is appropriate to the luxury market.

In metro Seattle, an agent who specializes in luxury waterfront properties always has his listings photographed from the water with a small yellow rubber ducky floating in one corner of the photograph. His listings are immediately identifiable and they catch attention and get a second look. You may forget his name, but you won't forget the rubber ducky. An agent in the San Francisco Bay area has a gift box delivered to prospects before a listing presentation. Inside, sellers find a brief video presentation on DVD about the agent's special marketing program for luxury homes, plus popcorn, cold drinks, and a note to enjoy the movie.

These are examples of fun ideas that are consistent with particular agents' styles. Things that help make them memorable. By all means implement ideas like these, but also remember that offering exceptional service is the best way to stand out.

Often when I speak to agents who aspire to work in the luxury home market they ask if one has to live in a million dollar house or drive a Mercedes to work with the affluent. The answer is absolutely not. While it helps to be memorable, it is not necessary to live a rich and famous lifestyle to work with that market segment. The affluent consumer is concerned about your competency – they want to know that you have the knowledge, tools, and expertise to help them accomplish their real estate objectives

One of my favorite real estate stories involves an agent from New Jersey. This young man told me that when he first decided to work in the upper tier he was really intimidated. He wasn't intimidated by the wealthy buyers and sellers that he knew he'd be working with. Instead, he was intimidated by other already successful luxury home agents. He was concerned about how well he could compete and about the fact that he didn't live an affluent lifestyle.

After some aggressive prospecting, he generated an opportunity to do a listing presentation on a wonderful country estate. He learned that he was the fourth and last presenter in the line-up. He did his homework to find out who his competitors for the listing would be. He knew the first agent would show up in her shiny new Mercedes. The second agent drove a nice BMW. The third agent would arrive with a car and driver. He told me he was totally intimidated by what he perceived to be their obvious success. He, on the other hand, would have to show up in his old -- but clean and serviceable – Volvo.

The day of his listing presentation came. He drove down the

private lane with its canopy of trees to the estate. Arriving at the house, he entered the huge stone drive in front of the house and pulled his old Volvo over as far as possible to one side. Then he climbed the steps to the big, hand-carved double doors with a huge brass knocker. He rapped on the door, and, sure enough, the owner himself opened the doors. The young agent said he stood there with his heart in his throat as he watched the owner's eyes go from him to the Volvo, back to him, back to the Volvo, and finally back to him. The agent stood there for what seemed like forever before the owner said, "Well, at last, a down-to-business automobile." At that moment, the agent said, he knew that the listing was his. Sure enough, he got the listing and the opportunity to demonstrate his competence. He also recognized that you don't have to live a wealthy lifestyle to work in the upper-tier market.

Use quality marketing materials. Slapdash materials, poor photocopies, and bad photographs have no place in luxury home marketing. Your materials should reflect the quality of the home you are marketing and the quality service you provide. If you aren't willing to invest in quality materials and professional photography, this may not be the market segment for you.

Network with other upper-tier agents. View your competition as a resource. As you become more and more involved in the luxury market, one of your greatest resources will be other agents who work in the upper-tier. Yes, you compete for prospects, but you will also find that there are lots of benefits which come from networking.

In many markets, luxury agents are formalizing their interactions and creating networking groups which tour each others' listings and provide written feedback, share wants and needs, provide vendor referrals to one another, and cooperate in a variety of other ways. You may want to establish or be part of such a group in the future. For starters, put some informal networking to work for you.

Here's how you can begin to enjoy the benefits of networking with other top upper-tier sales professionals in your market.

Start by identifying who is really listing and selling in the upper-tier. When you take the time to look closely at who is doing the business, you may find names you thought would be on the list are not, and others you weren't aware of who do lots of upscale business. Access your MLS information and do an analysis of who has the top properties in your market and create a list of luxury market agents. You've probably already done this as part of your competitive analysis.

If you have a luxury listing, send brochures and notes to agents on this list. Also send them a personal invitation to broker opens or invite them to preview your listings. When you co-broke with someone on the list, send a "nice to work with a pro" note. If you find a really interesting article which relates to the luxury market, send a copy with "thought you'd find this interesting" note.

Attend their broker opens and introduce yourself. Preview their properties (you need to know the inventory anyway). In short, work to build positive relationships with the agents who are doing business in the market segment where you want to work.

This will pay off in lots of ways. You will show and sell each other's listings. You'll discover there are certain agents with whom you enjoy working and who are eager to show and sell your listings, too. Over time, you may even want to refer expired listings (which you are about to lose) to a competitor, who is willing to reciprocate. At the very least, you'll ultimately find that you have a resource group to turn to when you need a vendor referral or other bit of information.

An example of how informal networking can become formalized is the *Luxury Home Marketing Group* in Raleigh/Durham (NC). Fourteen successful agents from a variety of companies have come together to create this networking group. They meet a couple of times a month and tour three properties listed by agents in the group. These are often situations where the listing agent would like group input on pricing, condition or other marketability factors.

The Raleigh group (informally they call themselves The Fab14) approaches this touring process with style. They use a white stretch Hummer to take them on tour. Of course there is a *Luxury Home Marketing Group* sign on the side of the vehicle. The limo wheels up to the subject properties, fourteen snappily dressed ladies pile out, tour the home and then off they go. As you can imagine, this creates lots of buzz in the neighborhoods they visit. Neighbors are calling home owners asking, "What was going on at your house this morning? What's the Luxury Home Marketing Group?" This kind of word of mouth creates visibility for the group and creates business for its members.

More important, are the results of the tours. Each agent provides written feedback to the listing agent. Suddenly, it isn't just the listing agent saying, we need to adjust the price or we really need to stage your home -- she is backed up by a group of the area's most knowledgeable upper-tier experts. After the tour the group meets for a brief working lunch and discusses market conditions and brainstorms wants and needs. This is business networking at its best.

There are a growing number of these professional networking groups around the country. Keller Williams in Atlanta has a luxury agent networking group within its company. In Houston, a group has just sprung up with agents from multiple brokerage firms participating. The Houston group is less about touring and more focused on education and identifying vendors and other important market resources. A new group of luxury agents from a variety of companies has formed in central Ohio. The members of these groups are agents who understand that cooperation can build everyone's business.

If the luxury market is one you are targeting, why not look for ways to network effectively with the competition? Cooperation is a strategy which can result in the individuals who are working together outperforming those who don't understand that networking can be a winning way to work. Yes, these agents are competitors, but they are also important resources for each other. Not only do they prosper through cooperation, their buyers and sellers also benefit from an improved level of service. That's a win-win for everyone.

Networking in more traditional ways also works. Hawaiian real estate agent Doug Shanefield was holding an open house when he met a man whose mother in New Jersey was in the market for an oceanfront home in Hawaii.

After a number of conversations about the prospect's requirements, Doug flew to New Jersey to present photographs and descriptions of a property he thought was a match for her desires. He even told her that he swam out to sea to check the view of the property from the water. Impressed with Shanefield and the home, the woman bought the house sight unseen.

Ten months later, the buyer called Shanefield asking if he could assist her with the sale of a cottage on Nantucket. A good networker, Shanefield quickly referred her to another agent specializing in luxury homes in Nantucket. The one bedroom cottage -- which happened to be on 65 acres -- sold for $19.5 million.

Make sure you are "farming" other luxury agents around the country so that you have an active referral network of others who are experts in the luxury niche.

Always be ethical. This is true regardless of price range, but it is too important to go unsaid. No matter how smart or clever or informed you are, if your word cannot be trusted or you act outside the best interests of those to whom you have a fiduciary responsibility, you will not be successful in the long term. Doing what is right should be one of your business principles. Recognize that integrity, authenticity, and trust are three principals which form the foundation of success.

Chapter Nine

Differentiating: Positioning Yourself as Unique and Better

In order to be unique and better able to meet the needs of the wealthy, you need to develop some special competencies.

Recognize architectural styles and terminology

Learn architectural styles and terminology. Your credibility suffers when you visit a potential listing or show a home and have no clue what architectural style or combination of styles the property is. There are numerous books available that can serve as quick references on architectural design. Go Online or to the architectural section in your local bookstore and you'll find publications that will give you an overview of architectural styles.

Several book suggestions are *What Style Is It: A Guide to American Architecture* by Poppeliers, Chambers, and Schwartz (published by John Wiley & Sons) or *A Field Guide to American Houses* by Virginia and Lee McAlester (published by Alfred A. Knopf). Another to consider is Identifying American Architecture by Blumenson (published by W.W. Norton & Company). These books are full of sketches and photographs illustrating specific styles. If you are still learning your architectural styles, you can drive up in front of a property, flip through the book, and in fairly short order figure out what style – or, as is sometimes the case, which combination of styles -- a property may be. Then, you can go in to visit with the seller with at least a bit of architectural knowledge.

Use the book as you preview properties; then, when you show them, you are prepared to talk about the architecture. After you've done this for six months, you'll find that the information has transferred itself from the book into your brain and you are becoming more knowledgeable about architectural styles.

The National Trust for Historic Preservation is also an excellent resource for learning more about home design. Their informative courses on architectural styles are open to real estate agents. See Chapter 15 of this book for more information on the National Trust.

Research leading architects –
Who designed a home can influence value

Research your area's leading architects, both past and present. I know you are a busy real estate agent juggling lots of things, but knowing which current architects are known for their residential designs and which architects are significant historically is very important for a variety of reasons. Get in the habit of asking, was your home designed by an architect? If so, do you know which one? Then use your favorite search engine to see if that architect might be significant enough to have a bearing on price or marketing. Who designed a home can have an impact on its value and even influence how you market it. Let me give you an illustration.

Working in Florida, particularly in the Palm Beach area, between World War I and World War II, there was an architect by the name of Addison Meisner. Meisner designed and built numerous properties for wealthy industrialists and was considered to be the premier architect in the United States in his time. He designed a fabulous house in Palm Beach for the owner and founder of the National Tea Company. As the story goes, when Meisner and the founder of the National Tea Company went to the property to do the final walk-through, they realized that the house had no staircase to the second floor. None. Obviously Meisner had to think fast to recover his credibility with his client. He proposed that that they add a fabulous turret containing a spiral staircase, which is what they did.

A few years ago, this property came on the market again. Imagine that you were one of the real estate agents competing for that listing. You sat down with the seller and said, "Thank you so much for the opportunity to talk to you about marketing your home. You know, this house has always fascinated me ever since I read the story about Meisner and the missing staircase." What just happened to your credibility? Do you also have a marketing hook? Could you build an entire promotional campaign for that house around the concept of the Meisner house with the missing staircase? It seems to me that you could really have some fun with that theme, get some free media exposure and generate a lot of "word of mouth" about that home. Does the fact that the house is a Meisner-designed home add value? Absolutely. The fact that it is the house with the missing staircase may add extra value for some prospects.

In some cases, prospects who wish to build custom homes or plan to redo the home they are purchasing may ask you to suggest architects to assist them.

To familiarize yourself with current architects and begin to develop a resource list:

- Use the Internet as a resource

- Most metro areas have local chapters of the American Institute of Architects. You can network with this group.

- As you get to know the luxury homebuilders in your market, ask them with which architects they commonly work.

- Watch your local newspaper and city magazines for features on luxury homes. Note the architects.

- Always ask sellers, "Was your home designed by an architect? If so, do you know which architect?"

- If you live in a large city, watch national publications like Architectural Digest for features on homes in your market. The architect and interior designers will almost always be credited.

To familiarize yourself with historic architects:

- Use the Internet as a resource, search engines can help you find information fast.

- Visit the library and/or local historic society and ask for information on well-known local architects from the past.

- Watch luxury home MLS listing information for references to specific architects from the past.

Delve into your area's history

Take the time to check out a book from your local library, skim it, and learn a bit about your community's history. This will give you some great ideas for creative marketing or what I call romancing your listing. Sometimes even knowing more about your area's history than your competitors know will help you win a listing. At least, that's what a Maryland agent discovered when she went on a listing presentation in Chevy Chase, located in suburban Washington, D.C., inside the beltway. It is one of Washington's more desirable, close-in suburbs; however, when Chevy Chase was developed at the turn of the century it was not in easy commuting range. In fact, it was considered so far away that the developers positioned it as a weekend or summer community. Realizing that they needed to be creative to sell their development, the first thing they did was put in a pretty little man-made lake. They added a park area with places to picnic, a gazebo, and bandstand. They then developed their building lots. The important additional investment was a little electric trolley that ran from Chevy Chase into Washington, D.C. Then they began to promote their development to the affluent households in Washington. They said, "Come on up to Chevy Chase. Bring the family. You can picnic around the lake and use the paddleboats. When the sun begins to go down, we'll have a concert in the bandstand, you can dance on the dance floor, and we'll have fireworks over the lake. Of course, while you're there, let us show you our lots." Sounds like the pitch for a land development today, doesn't it?

Over time, they sold the lots in Chevy Chase. This was around the turn of the twentieth century, so a lot of wonderful sprawling Victorian houses with big porches were built in Chevy Chase. A couple of years ago, one of those original houses went on the market. One of the agents who had an opportunity to go out and do a listing presentation on this home met with the sellers and said, "I am just delighted to have the opportunity to talk to you about listing your home. This is one of my favorite houses in Chevy Chase. I've always admired the big wrap-around porch. In fact, this is one of the very first houses built on the lake."

The sellers looked at her and said, "Wait a minute, what lake?" The lake is no longer there; it has been gone for decades. The property became so valuable that at some point along the way it was filled in and built over. The agent said, "Don't you know the history of Chevy Chase?" And the sellers said, "No, we just moved here with the last administration, and we don't know much about this area."

So, the agent told them the story about the development of Chevy Chase. They said, "Anyone who knows that much about this area is the person we want listing our home. You've got the listing." Certainly, the agent has some marketing hooks for romancing that property. It may seem like a small thing, but the more you know about your area's history, the more likely you are to find some interesting and effective ways to promote listings. Stories are effective marketing tools.

Develop your knowledge of upper-tier builders and developers

In some markets there is an opportunity to work with residential developers and new homebuilders by representing them in the marketing of building lots and homes. Even if builders will not list with you, if you are just getting started in the upper-tier, it may be worth your time to volunteer to hold a new home open for a custom builder or advertise a builder's listings in order to attract prospective high-ticket buyers.

Getting to know the custom homebuilders in your market may also create opportunities for referrals. If one of their buyers has a home to sell, ask the builder to refer the listing to you.

Another important reason to be familiar with upper priced new home inventory is that new homes compete with resale listings. Many buyers look at both. You need to preview the properties, both new and resale, which are competitive with your listings.

You need to be able to talk intelligently to the buyer who is considering a new home and be prepared show them the best available properties for their needs.

Comparables can sometimes be difficult to find when you are dealing with an expensive custom home. Turning to the new home market will sometimes give you the best comparables based on amenities, quality of construction, size, or other factors.

Recognize that who built a home can sometimes make a difference in value. There are probably builders in your market who build with sufficient quality that you add value to their homes, and other builders whose construction causes you to reduce value for their homes. You need to know which are which.

Recognize amenities that add value

According to the National Association of Homebuilders research report, What 21st Century Homebuyers Want, buyers of $350,000 new homes (these are homes priced above the median price) want 3000 square feet, four or more bedrooms, three or more baths, and three-car garages. Kitchens with island work areas and hard surface counter tops such as Corian and granite are on the list along with high ceilings, crown moldings, French doors, skylights, and central vacuum systems. Special room requirements include sunrooms, media rooms, and home offices. Porches/decks/patios and security systems also rank high on the list of desirable or required features.

While, it is safe to assume these features are usually expected by the homebuyer above $350,000, the luxury buyer wants more and can afford the features that support their lifestyles. Gourmets and those who entertain may want super-sized professional gas ranges, large temperature-controlled wine rooms or full wine cellars (with case and bottle storage), furniture-quality kitchen cabinets, and large butler's pantries for storing china, crystal, serving pieces, and flatware. Wealthy households with full staff may want gourmet kitchens that are separate from the family living area or multiple kitchens -- including a mini-kitchen with coffee bar in the master bedroom. Fully equipped outdoor kitchens with grilling areas are gaining popularity in warmer climates, and catering kitchens are often on the must-have list for those who entertain large groups and want their main gourmet kitchen to remain pristine when they entertain.

Popular spa bathroom features include heated floors, steam showers, saunas, and sitting room/dressing room areas as well as spa/massage or yoga/meditation areas. Special purpose closets for furs, ball gowns, or luggage may be positive features. Home gyms, resistance lap-pools, tennis courts, and putting greens may be desired by those who can afford them. Home theatres are increasingly common and built-in plasma-screen TVs are showing up in media rooms, bedrooms and in kitchens. Entire homes are wired with sophisticated music systems. Maid/staff quarters, guesthouses, and pool cabanas may also be on some buyers' must-have lists.

Many buyers have strong preferences in architectural style. Gardens may be a significant amenity for some buyers. Being able to enjoy a view of water, mountains, or a city skyline may also be important. Security systems and safe rooms may also be desired. One of the most creative luxury features I've encountered recently is the use of warming drawers (usually a kitchen amenity for keeping food hot) used in the bathroom for keeping towels toasty warm and ready to use.

Construction and finish-out features that are gaining in popularity include window glass with anti-dirt glaze, European-built working windows with solid metal hardware, single-family home elevators, solar panel roofing that looks like slate, heated floors, and special ceiling treatments ranging from coffered to Trompe l'oeil painted ceilings.

There is not one list of key features for luxury homebuyers— remember these are the people who can afford a home that is customized for the way they live, work, and entertain. What is important is quality and luxury. Also recognize that certain construction materials, brands of appliances and fixtures may be selling points and may make a difference in pricing.

Ask your buyer prospects what special features are essential and what other features are desirable to them. The more you know about their lifestyle, the easier it will be to find just the right home for them. Also remember to ask your sellers what features they've most enjoyed about the home they are selling. Chances are these may be some of the key features the new buyer will be excited about as well.

Pay attention to interior design and landscape design

You don't need to be an expert in interior design and landscape design, but you do need to know when they add value to a property or make the property desirable for a particular market segment.

An agent in the Carolinas told me that she listed a property with one of about 50 antique camellia gardens in the world. She said, "I didn't even know what a camellia looked like until I listed the house, but I knew that for some small segment of the market that garden was going to add value." She worked with the owner to develop a strategy to reach the international gardening community. She sold the house to someone who paid a premium and for whom the garden was probably more important than the home. To that buyer, the value was in the garden. Knowing that these things can matter and asking the right questions so that you can take advantage of special opportunities will help separate you from competitors.

To keep current on trends in decor and landscaping and to monitor what new amenities and features luxury homeowners desire, periodically scan publications such as Sales and Marketing Ideas (a bi-monthly publication of the National Sales and Marketing Council of the National Association of Home Builders) and shelter publications like Architectural Digest, Dwell, House and Garden, Elle Décor, and Traditional Home.

Learn to handle the multi-level sale

Often in the higher price ranges you will encounter players other than the buyer and seller. You may work with an implementer, a screener, and invariably (but not unique to the upper tier) the ubiquitous deal killer. Let's look at each of these roles.

The implementer supervises the service. An example of this would be a trustee. Assume a property goes into trust and it becomes the trustee's responsibility to get that property sold. The trustee is not the owner. He or she simply has the task of initiating and managing the service that you're going to provide. In some cases the implementer may be given responsibility for negotiating the deal. In other cases, an implementer is simply responsible for selecting an agent, getting the property listed, and turning the contract over to someone else to negotiate. An implementer has no emotional attachment to the property. Implementers are judged on bottom line performance. How quickly was the property sold, for how much money, and were the proceeds distributed as they were suppose to be, based on the terms and conditions of the trust? As a result they will look to you to get results. Generally you will know when you are dealing with an implementer

I did a luxury home marketing program several years ago in the Cayman Islands and the agents attending explained to me that they frequently work with implementers. Often representatives of wealthy individuals will come to the islands to buy and sell residential real estate for their clients or employers. Properties are often purchased in corporate names and go immediately into pools of luxury rentals. The owners may never see the property because they're not buying the property to live in; they're buying it because of tax shelter needs or other financial considerations. In these situations, the implementer selected the property and negotiated the transaction. So, depending upon where you are and what kind of a market you are in, you may interact with an implementer.

The screener is another player working with a different agenda. The screener is usually brought into a transaction by a high profile buyer to maintain confidentiality. Many markets have well known business people, sports stars, or celebrities from the media, entertainment, or music fields. These individuals are often at a disadvantage when negotiating to buy a residential property and are concerned about security and privacy. If Bill Gates or Julia Roberts wants to buy your home, how willing are you going to be to negotiate price? You're likely to assume the attitude that they can afford to pay full price.

The screener may be a business manager, relative, or other trusted individual who is given a description of the desired property or a list of criteria. The screener is asked to screen agents, select one or more with whom to work, and then screen properties.

The screener narrows the property alternatives to just a few and the potential buyer then looks at those homes (often Online through photos and videos) and makes the selection. At this point, the screener may become an implementer or hand off the negotiation of the transaction to another representative of the celebrity.

Unless you are prequalifying prospects at first contact (a good idea), you may not always realize that you are working with a screener. If you suspect that someone is a screener, ask. It is not necessary to know for whom they are screening, but it will often explain why the showing and decision process may seem to be proceeding differently. Recognize that when you're working with screeners, they have veto power. First, they're screening to find the right agent and they can choose you or not. They also have veto power over the properties. Their motivation is three-fold: finding an agent with whom both screener and principal will feel comfortable, finding homes that match the selection criteria, and, of course, maintaining confidentiality.

An agent specializing in country property in South Carolina was working with a buyer prospect and after several property showings decided that the man was screening for someone. Rapport was good and when the agent asked, the gentleman confided, on condition of confidentiality, that he was screening for a well-known singer.

Several days later they looked at a property that was listed by a competing broker who was present for the showing. Something the screener said alerted the listing broker to the fact that the screener was looking for this celebrity. Later that week, the other broker ran an ad in the local newspaper that identified the celebrity by saying even so-and-so looks at our listings. The screener called his agent to say, "You've been great and you've shown me some properties which were real possibilities, but confidentiality has been breached along with her ability to negotiate. In fact, she said not only are we not going to buy in South Carolina, she told me not to waste my time looking in North Carolina." Confidentially is key when dealing with celebrities directly or with their screeners.

Another frequent player in the luxury market is the deal killer. This player often pops up in the negotiation stage. One obvious deal killer is the attorney, but others can play the role as well. A number of years ago there was an article in a national publication about business managers for the affluent. One of the business managers interviewed described a situation involving one of his clients who is a high profile actress. It seems she had found a house that she just absolutely had to have. It was listed for more than $1 million. She contracted for it. When the business manager discovered this, he stepped in and renegotiated the contract. In this case he didn't kill the transaction, but he did change it substantially. Deal killers are generally motivated by wanting to improve the deal. And, as was the case with the business manager, they are often not present at the beginning of the transaction; they are invited in or interject themselves later in the process.

Probably the most common deal killers which real estate agents encounter are not in the upper tier, they are in the first time homebuyer market -- mom and dad. Parents frequently interject themselves into their children's transactions. They want to be certain the kids are getting a good buy. To understand the concept of the deal killer, just think about mom and dad and the first time homebuyer, and you'll get the picture.

When the deal killer shows up, just be prepared to make the sale for a second time, explaining the benefits and educating the new player on the realities of the market.

Better yet, smoke out the deal killer in advance by asking this question early in your interaction with a buyer or seller, "Is there anyone you'll be turning to for information or advice as you make your buying/selling decision?" Be careful not to imply that they are not making their own decision by using the phrase, "as you make your buying/selling decision." If your prospect tells you he or she will be consulting with a tax advisor, attorney, business manager or other individual, you are forewarned and can often involve the prospective deal killer early in the transaction and "make the sale" to them earlier in the process, avoiding a last minute deal-killing confrontation.

Refine your valuation skills

Your ability to peg the price at which a unique custom home will sell is important to your credibility and success. Pricing upper end homes properly is more difficult than pricing less expensive homes for which there are many comparables. You will be concerned with size, condition, amenities, functionality, location, market activity – the same things you look at when pricing any property; but even very experienced agents can sometimes find valuing unique custom homes challenging.

An agent in the Southwest faced with pricing a custom-built 45,000-square-foot home with in- and outdoor pools, guest house, staff quarters, and an amazing list of other features, actually went outside her market area to find comparably sized properties and then adjusted for market price differences as well as for other features. Even looking in other markets, the number of 45,000-square-foot homes is limited.

A number of years ago, when the market was in a severe down cycle in parts of New England, it was not uncommon for an agent preparing a market analysis on a luxury home to use the subject property as its own comparable. The agent would look at the last time the property sold, calculate how much the market prices had changed in that price range (in this case the change was a decline) and then apply that percentage to adjust the previous sales price to a current value. Going out of the area or using the subject property as its own comparable are extreme techniques, but are sometimes necessary in the luxury market.

Nor is it uncommon for a prelisting appraisal to be part of the pricing process. This appraisal can be especially important when an agent feels the seller may have unrealistic expectations about price. If you do a prelisting appraisal, be sure that you select an appraiser who is knowledgeable about the general price range of the home and the geographic area. Not every appraiser is knowledgeable about luxury property. Also be certain the appraiser knows the appraisal is for resale rather than refinance purposes.

When you are ordering the prelisting appraisal, negotiate with the appraiser to allow you and your seller, at your discretion, to provide the appraisal to the buyer's lender without having to pay a second fee. While the buyer's lender will certainly order their own appraisal, a good pre-listing appraisal becomes a resource for the lender's appraiser and may help establish reasonable value in support of the contract price. Generally the sellers pay for this pre-listing appraisal and it should be ordered in their name.

Occasionally in the upper tier you'll come across a home with a feature that is so unique that it is difficult to price, or so unusual it may impair your ability to sell the home, in which case it becomes a price-reducing feature. One day during the break at a training session for luxury home agents in Los Angeles, an agent told me he was in the process of listing a home, but was in a bit of a quandary about pricing. His concern centered around one of the home's features, an underground shooting range. He felt that for most prospects it would be a negative. He joked about doing some target marketing with licensed gun owners, but admitted that he didn't think that was the best approach. As he described the shooting range to me, I realized that it was basically just a big soundproof room with sliding targets and probably some holes in the wall.

As we talked, it dawned on both of us that the shooting range could easily be transformed into a feature that would add tremendous value to a home in Los Angeles. You have probably already guessed what we came up with. The big empty, soundproof room with its targets removed could easily be marketed as a recording studio. He took a lemon of a feature (one which had limited appeal) and made lemon meringue pie.

No matter how effective you are at pricing property, you will invariably encounter the seller who laments, "My house must be worth more!"

A number of agents have told me that, when they encounter this objection, they ask the sellers, "If you were going to buy your home today, what would you pay for it?" Then, they tell them what the monthly payment and qualifying income would be at that price. Sellers will often say, "Oh my gosh! I had no idea," especially if they've been in their house for a while. This opens the door to explaining how too a high price will limit the number of potential buyers and lengthen the marketing time.

If you've got a seller who still insists their house is worth more, and you've negotiated, and you've looked at the statistics and you just can't get together on price, try the Buyer for the Afternoon approach. This doesn't work every time, but it's worth a try as a way to give your seller a dose of market reality. The script below works well with business owners, corporate executives, and self-employed professionals. Just tweak it to match your seller's situation.

Develop a script that creates a dialogue along these lines, "You're in business. Let me ask you a question. In your business, would you ever bring a new product or service into the marketplace without doing some research on how your competitors are pricing similar products or services?"

The usual response is, "Of course not."

"Well, isn't your house one of the most important products that you're going to sell this year?"

"That's right."

"So, since we're not in agreement as to the price and since your home is a very important product, I'm going to propose that we do some price comparison, just like you do in your own business. I know you're busy, but since pricing your home correctly is of critical importance, I think we need to invest a few hours in pricing research. I'd like for us to go out and look at a couple of properties in the price range where you think your house should be listed and a couple of properties in the price range where I think your house should be listed. Then, we'll sit down again and talk price. Is that reasonable?"

Usually your seller will agree.

Take your seller to look at two cream of the crop, absolutely best properties in the price range where they want to list, which obviously is higher than the price range where you want to list.

Then look at the two best cream puff properties in the price range where you think the home should be listed. Make sure you have previewed these properties and select carefully. This dose of market reality should help you in your negotiation of a reasonable list price. It doesn't always work, but as a last resort before either taking an overpriced listing or walking away, it's worth trying.

To implement this technique, you must be knowledgeable enough about competing properties to be able to select the best properties to look at with your seller. This emphasizes the importance of previewing the entire inventory. It also puts you in the position of asking to show a listing to someone who may not be a valid prospect. Here's a situation where networking with other luxury home agents pays off. Explain to the listing agent that you are doing pricing research with a client and that you would like to preview (as opposed to show) the home and will bring your client with you. Indicate that you will be happy to provide written feedback from your perspective and share your client's comments if they would be useful to the lister in working with his or her seller. Also volunteer to reciprocate when the other agent would like to do something similar. A good agent will usually see value in this and be able to schedule an appointment for you.

Thanks to the Internet, you can also implement this technique by doing your pricing research Online. Obviously, you'll choose the properties carefully. "Tour" these cream-of-the-crop properties by viewing the property Websites, look at the photographs, view any videos, and review the property information. One advantage to doing your pricing research in this manner is that if the other listing agents have done a good job, you'll see all the strong points of the competing properties.

Be an information source for the affluent

As your reputation as a pricing expert in the luxury home market grows, you may get a call from an owner who says, "You've been referred to me as a luxury home expert. I am not selling my house, I am taking out a loan for my business and my banker is requiring personally liability. I am working with my accountant to prepare information on my personal assets and I need a market valuation for my home. Can you help me?" Your answer should be affirmative because this is an opportunity for possible future business or to ask for a referral.

Agents in the upper-tier market will usually develop extensive resource lists. Those who are new to the area often ask about sources for services including (but not limited to):

- Jumbo mortgage loans
- Interior decorators
- Painters, carpet cleaners, and other service people
- Antique and oriental rug dealers
- Craftspeople who do stonework, faux finishes, or hand-scraped inlaid hardwood floors
- Landscape designers, pool companies, or deck designers
- Caterers, party planners, personal chefs
- Private airports with hangers for housing planes
- Marinas and private airports
- Housecleaning, pool, and plant care services
- Nanny finders or daycare services
- Personal trainers, massage therapists, hairstylists, day spas, or exercise facilities
- Sources for butlers and home managers

In short, your affluent clients will often turn to you for a long list of resource recommendations. Develop contacts in these areas and network with them. The painter who is redoing a home before it goes on the market can be a source of referrals; the marina owner who is helping a client sell a boat before relocating can give you a recommendation that leads to a listing. Interact with others who work with the wealthy. It will pay off.

Serving as a source of information is also an aspect of providing exceptional service. Some brokerage firms that specialize in the upscale market are offering concierge services through affiliation with national or international concierge companies. These firms provide extensive services, from travel assistance to special requests for theatre and sporting event tickets, limo arrangements, shopping, etc.

As an example, this level of service is offered by EDJ Realty, a boutique real estate firm specializing in luxury real estate, founded by Institute member DeShawn Snow in metropolitan Atlanta (GA). The company's tagline, "Exceptional Service for Exquisite Living," is built on Snow's simple philosophy: "Our clients deserve the best, and that is what we give them. We strive to fulfill every wish with reliable and reputable service, professional advice, discretion, and close personal attention."

For Snow, outstanding service has been the key component since she founded the company: "We would arrange for delivery of furniture and cars, coordinate with other service providers (audio/video, interior design), stock the refrigerator with their favorite items, purchase pots/pans, other kitchen items, etc."

Snow assigned her business manager to oversee these special projects, but when she began putting systems in place to improve productivity, she decided to contract her firm's exceptional service to an outside provider. They key, though, was finding a company that she could trust to provide the type of red carpet service that is the very essence of her firm's identity: "EDJ Realty is built as much upon exceptional service to clients as on the quality of the homes we market and sell," says Snow.

After an exhaustive search, Snow decided to contract with an existing concierge company which would brand the concierge service with Snow's company name. "Everything has my EDJ Realty brand," said Snow. "My clients place a phone call or log in through our Website to access the concierge. This is totally turnkey for me. The benefit to me is the client is always calling EDJ Realty Concierge services to access the service, so we have top-of-mind awareness!"

The concierge company keeps an extensive 125 question personal profile on each one of Snow's clients. "It's often the smallest details that make the biggest difference when standing out from the crowd. Everything from the client's pet's name to what temperature they like their bottled water to be. To us, it's all about the details," said Snow.

Snow offers free hours of concierge service to her clients depending on the price of the home purchased or sold. The full-service concierge can handle travel planning, reservations, weekend getaways, chartering a yacht or jet, or whatever the client needs. There are over 300 concierges in 80 cities world wide in the company Snow selected as her vendor.

"This is much more than the traditional real estate concierge service that just helps with utilities and makes referrals," said Snow. "For example, if I sold a second home to a client, they can use the service to have someone stock the place prior to their arrival. This service will be free to the client; they just need to pay for the groceries. Or if someone wanted to rent a red Lamborghini with their favorite bottle of wine in the seat, EDJ Realty Concierge can handle that as well!"

Snow recently acquired an exclusive listing for a gated community of eight homes, each priced at $2 million or more. She is offering each homeowner 50 hours of concierge services, which means that the community can now offer concierge services as an amenity. Snow is providing double value – the builder/developer benefits as do the homebuyers.

Snow frequently works with and understands the needs of professional athletes and entertainers. "Most of my clients would pay to have someone to take care of these types of services anyway. By offering it as part of EDJ Realty's services, it saves them time and money. I have a few ball players I am working with who plan on purchasing homes in a couple of months, and they all love the fact that I handle all the details."

Note for Institute members: Members who are interested in offering concierge services may be able to do so through a concierge marketing partner of The Institute. See the Members Only section of www.LuxuryHomeMarketing.com.

Build visibility and credibility by being a resource to the media

With some creativity and effort, you can add your name to the list of contacts reporters use when working on stories about luxury real estate. The keys to success are reaching out to the media with important information and understanding how you can help them do their jobs more effectively.

Identify specific media targets. Don't try to reach the entire media world. Focus on a target list of no more than a dozen news outlets. You'll probably want to include print, broadcast and Online publications. Then, take the time to compile the names of the specific reporters and editors you want to reach.

Use valuable information as a hook. One especially effective way to make an initial contact is to provide market statistics or other important information about what's happening in the luxury market. For instance, if the high rise condo segment is awash with international buyers or a particular price range is outperforming the market as a whole, a reporter may appreciate the story tip. Be sure to include a letter introducing yourself, explain that you work in the luxury home market, mention your specific areas of expertise (high rise condos, suburban waterfront, homes priced at $5 million plus…) and volunteer to be a resource for them. "How can I help you?" is an important question. You can phone, but remember that writers are often on deadline and so keep any phone conversation you initiate short.

Mary Umberger, a high profile reporter who covers the real estate beat with the Chicago Tribune, says what endears her to a real estate agent source is the agent's willingness to state an opinion about what's happening in the market and to provide real information and examples. She's also interested in agents who can connect her with what she calls real people. "There's no shortage of agents to talk to," she says. "What's gold to me is an agent who will put me with a client who has an interesting story."

What's surprising is that Umberger complains that only one in three agents she contacts when working on a story will call her back. The ones who don't call are missing the opportunity for additional visibility and credibility in the marketplace. When the press calls, be responsive.

Build your expertise. If you want to position yourself as a media source, here's a short checklist to ensure that you can help the press and add value to their stories.
Can you provide ideas for timely stories?

- Do you have market knowledge that will add credibility to stories?
- Can you provide interesting "sound bites" and quotes?
- Can you offer solid statistics to illustrate what's happening in the market?
- Can you suggest a local tie-in for a national real estate story?
- Can you pass on interesting articles on hot industry topics from trade publications and blogs?
- Can you offer a checklist or list of fast facts to interest readers?
- Can you make introductions? If the reporter is looking for homebuyers or sellers to interview, first get permission from your clients, and then pass the contact info to the reporter.

As you build your relationships with the press, leverage the media coverage you generate. Set up an "In the news" section on your Website and post the articles quoting you there. It's a great way to gain credibility with prospects who are reviewing your site

Here's an example of the kind of news release you might use. This is a press release we provided to our Institute members for them to customize and use in their local markets. The release reports on a U.S. home sale record set in May of 2007. When national news like this is reported, be the first in your market to take it and give it a local twist.

PRESS RELEASE

(CONTACT: YOUR NAME AND CONTACT INFO)

For immediate release

Record US residential sale breaks $100 million mark

**Heiress sells 40-acre "building lot"
in New York's Hamptons
to financial mogul for $103 million**

(City, State and Date) The cloud over the current residential real estate market has a silver lining. The upper-tier market continues to boom, as evidenced by the record-breaking sale of a residential property in East Hampton (NY) for $103 million.

The new sale was supposed to be hush-hush; but, the news was quickly out that Schlumberger Oil fortune heiress Adelaide de Menil and her husband Ted Carpenter had sold the pricey ocean front property to Ron Baron, founder of Baron Funds Investment Company. The transaction breaks the previous record for the most expensive home sold in the U.S. which was set in 2004, by the sale of Revlon Chairman Ron Perelman's Palm Beach estate for $70 million.

Although the sale in the Hamptons is a new U.S. record, the world record residential sale was set this year by Sheikh Hamad of Qatar, who purchased a flat in London for £100 million British pounds (about $200 million in U.S. dollars).

"By comparison, the most expensive home sold last year in _____ was $_____," according to (YOUR NAME, of YOUR FIRM). "QUOTE FROM YOU ABOUT YOUR LOCAL LUXURY MARKET.)

"Although the US housing market slipped overall in 2006, the luxury market has continued to boom, as a result of rising wealth at the top of the demographic pyramid," said Laurie Moore-Moore, Founder of the Dallas-based Institute for Luxury Home Marketing. "Sales of homes priced at $5 million and above jumped 11% last year and rose a staggering 31% in the first quarter of 2007, according to new research by Vancouver-based DataQuick."

"At least five US sellers are so optimistic that the luxury home market will stay strong that they've priced their homes at more than $100 million," said

Moore-Moore. "The chances are good that Baron won't be king of the residential hill for long, we may see a new record in the next 18 months or so."

Leading the pack as the priciest estate is "The Pinnacle," under construction at the members-only Yellowstone Club in Montana, and offered for sale by the club's developer, Tim Blixseth, for $155 million. The four other highest priced homes include Saudi Prince Bandar's estate in Aspen (CO), priced at $135 million; "Fleur De Lys", a Los Angeles (CA) property priced at $125 million; Donald Trump's $125 million Palm Beach (FL) re-do; and the $100 million estate known as "Tranquility," at Lake Tahoe (NV).

The priciest home currently on the market locally is $_____, said (YOUR LAST NAME. ADD MORE DETAILS)

"One interesting fact about the record-setting New York sale," added Moore-Moore, "is that Baron didn't want the existing homes on the property. So, they were removed for his convenience, leaving him with a fabulous site for building his custom home." The houses were donated to the nearby community for use as city buildings.

###

Build credibility with designations

Earn designations because they help reinforce your positioning as an expert. If you work with a consumer who is a C.P.A., an M.D., or a PhD, they value their own designations, recognize what it takes to earn one, and respect other individuals who also have designations. A luxury home marketing designation has value, as do other designations that also help build skills and enhance credibility. The Certified Luxury Home Marketing Specialist designation (CLHMS) from the Institute for Luxury Home Marketing gives you added credibility with the affluent. (www.LuxuryHomeMarketing.com)

Working with The National Association of Realtors® on the development of a report titled, "Recruiting and Retaining Highly Successful Agents," I was involved in research that included a statistical analysis of what characteristics of top agents translated into additional income. In this study, the two items that had the strongest statistical correlation to making more money were NAR's Certified Residential Specialist designation (CRS) and a high level of technology usage. Obviously, this is an example of the value of a designation. The CRS skill-based training and the member network combine to make those who hold this designation more successful.

In addition to the CLHMS and CRS designations, you may want to consider other designations which may be helpful in the luxury market segment. If your market includes resort homes, NAR also offers the "Resort and Second Home Property Specialist" designation. If you're targeting the International buyer and seller, consider NAR's Certified International Property Specialist (CIPS) designation. Find more about NAR designations by visiting www.Realtor.org)

For additional expertise in new home construction, check out the Certified New Home Specialist designation (CNHS) and the accompanying Residential Construction Certified accreditation offered by Dennis Walsh & Associates by going to www.SellNewHomes.com.

Author's Note: Each day of the Institute's two-day CLHMS designation training course may qualify for one elective course credit for the CRS designation (for a potential total of two elective credits). See our course schedule at www.LuxuryHomeMarketing for details on which scheduled dates provide credit toward the CRS designation.

Differentiate yourself:
Six steps to finding and promoting your uniqueness

In today's competitive market you must differentiate yourself from others who work in the upper tier. To do that, you must be able to capture consumers' attention, pique their interest, and create a willingness to work with you so they will say, "Yes, you're the agent for me." It's the classic advertising formula of Attention, Interest, Desire, and Action. Done well, it works. The challenge is implementing the AIDA formula effectively -- especially in an industry where the consumer does not always perceive that there is a difference in real estate agents and the services they deliver.

To maximize your success, you must differentiate yourself. Simply stated, you need to convince the consumer that you are unique and better able to meet his or her needs than your competitors are. If you've focused on developing the special competencies we've discussed above, you've taken a big step in the right direction. Now it's time to zero in on how to build the awareness of rich buyers and sellers that you are unique and better. Here are six steps to help you set yourself apart from the crowd with a unique value proposition:

1. Understand the customer's needs. What do affluent buyers and sellers expect from you? How do you add value to the process of buying and selling? How do your services measure up? Ask your clients about their expectations of you and how you measured up, then listen and learn.

2. Be an Expert. Keep your upper-end market knowledge current, master the complexities of the buying/selling process, and polish your communication skills. It's one thing to convince the consumer that you are unique and better able to meet their his or her needs. You must also deliver on that promise. Competence is the foundation upon which you must build your business.

3. Discover your unique abilities. You may be a powerful

negotiator. Perhaps you know the market inventory better than anyone else. You may be masterful in listing properties and implementing luxury home marketing plans but prefer not to work with buyers. Maybe you specialize in luxury resort properties, golf communities, equestrian properties, downtown condos and co-ops, or know more about jumbo mortgage financing than anybody else in your office. New homes may be your specialty. Relocation buyers or high-end corporate listings may be your focus. Ask yourself what you like to do and what you do best. Sell your strengths. The things that make you unique also make you marketable.

4. Define your ideal target customer. It is difficult to be all things to all people. Look at your unique abilities and then ask yourself what customer groups need those abilities most. Analyze the opportunities in your market and then match your skills with the market segments that need what you can offer.

Remember, if you don't choose your market, your market will choose you. For instance, you might do a good job for a first time homebuyer, who refers you to a friend who also sends you business. Before you know it, first-timers are taking most of your time and representing most of your business. That's fine, if that's what you love doing. But if you'd really rather be listing upper-priced homes and have the skills to do so, you've missed the opportunity to develop your ideal market.

5. Put your uniqueness into words. Write down your unique abilities and then list how these abilities translate into benefits for the market segments you are targeting. Take the home-buyers' and sellers' points of view and answer their qestion "What does that mean to me?" For instance, you might write, "My strong negotiation skills and track record of selling luxury

homes for an average of 99% of the asking price mean sellers can depend on me to help them get the best possible price for their homes." Writing down what makes you special helps you clearly define it.

6. Condense your uniqueness into a "positioning" statement (Try to sell the sizzle, not the steak!). Translate your uniqueness into a single statement that "positions" you in the way you wish to be perceived. Then use that statement or unique value proposition to help create your special brand. This will help you capture the attention and interest of prospects and give them a clear reason why they might desire to work with you.

Think about some of the positioning statements or branding campaign themes used by other products and services and you'll get the idea. Club Med's "The Antidote for Civilization" or BMW's "The Ultimate Driving Machine" are short but powerful messages. Don't be afraid to use humor. For example, "100 Pipers Scotch ... Makes Bagpipes Sound Like Music" is almost certain to stop you and make you smile. Ernst & Young conveys the extensiveness of their consulting services with the line, "From thought to finish." Dell Computer clearly puts strategy and benefits into this line, "Total accountability. On-site, Online, on the phone. Easy as Dell." Yellow Freight Service keeps their delivery promise short but strong, "Yes we can." Paul Stuart Menswear reminds us that our clothing makes a statement with two words, "Say Something." The Senior PGA Golf Tour gives us a reason to tune in to watch their matches, "These Guys Are Good." And, Hummer has sparked sales with "Hummer -- Like Nothing Else."

It's a bit harder to find positioning statements in real estate. But here are a few to jump-start your thinking. A team of

California Realtors® who use a Q&A radio talk show to position themselves as the experts in their market use the line, "Bakersfield's Most Listened to Realtors®." Do you immediately know the specialties of "Waterfront Lifestyle Specialist," or "Call the We Get It SOLD Sisters"?

In Longboat Key (FL) agent Cheryl Loeffler uses the line "Select Cheryl with a Sea" to reinforce her name as well as her waterfront expertise. To expand on the positioning line and underscore the benefits of working with her, Cheryl's marketing materials go on to say, "She's called Cheryl with a Sea. But it's more than just a play on words. It describes why Cheryl is uniquely equipped to handle your real estate needs. Her own experiences as a Longboat Key resident and Realtor allow her to emphasize features that buyers desire: scenic views, beach access, and leisure opportunities, to name a few. She uses insights gained from her business and personal life to design the ideal marketing strategies for your property."

Define how you are unique, develop your positioning statement, and use it in your advertising, on your business card, and in your marketing presentations. Include it in your voice mail message, in your e-mail signature, and on your stationery. When you understand your uniqueness and convey it to targeted prospect groups in a benefit-oriented way, you will capture the affluent prospects' attention and also create interest and the desire to work with you. Remember the AIDA formula? All that's left is Action – ask for their business and chances are good, they'll say, "Yes!"

Chapter Ten

Finding Rich Buyers and Rich Sellers

Farming

Create a farming program (yes, farming works in the luxury price ranges). Just be sure the farming pieces are consistent with the price range. Think quality, quality, quality. In addition to traditional farming approaches like just sold and just listed cards, tweak traditional farming techniques to match the luxury market. Here is a brief list of ideas to spark your thinking about farming in the luxury home market.

- Instead of recipe cards and mass market farming newsletters, send frequent market update reports with statistical information about the local upper-tier real estate market. Make sure your mailing has a quality look. Use charts and graphs.

- Set up a special luxury market section on your Webpage. Post your statistical market updates and other information relevant to the luxury buyer and seller Online. Feature your upper-priced listings in this section of your Webpage.

- Send your luxury market updates to the community association newsletter editors of luxury home communities.

- Just breaking in to the upper-tier? Volunteer to sit on other agents' higher priced open houses in return for the chance to meet prospects – this will help you break into the entry level luxury home market or help you recover if your business slides into a slump.

- Use your leftover luxury home property information sheets and brochures. Mail them out with stickers that say, "Another Sally Salespro listing SOLD!"

- Take your own or your office successes and turn them into story postcards that present a real estate challenge and explain how your expertise or firm's approach created the solution.

- Network, network, network. Trust and estate attorneys, private bankers, stock brokers, divorce lawyers, golf pros, luxury car dealers, CPAs, and country club membership directors are examples of those who are in a position to refer business to you. Remember networking with other agents who work the upper priced market is also very important.

- Look for ways to interact with the affluent. If you want to get involved in your community you can contribute while creating relationships that may result in referrals. Volunteer at local museums, get involved with the arts, and participate in charity events. Establish the relationships first, and then farm the resulting contacts that you've made.

- If you've chosen a luxury neighborhood to farm, offer to sponsor the community's Website -- coordinate with the community association to post important announcements, the PDF version of their newsletter, membership information, or other relevant material that will attract residents to the community (YOUR) site.

- If you specialize in a segment or segments of the luxury market, such as golf course properties, equestrian properties, or yacht club residences, take time to learn about the related lifestyle. Search out related lifestyle Websites and identify the services and other resources people enjoying this lifestyle might also need. In short, work to make yourself an expert in the lifestyle these properties represent. Reflect this expertise on your Website with relevant links, participate in key events (boat shows, golf tournaments, etc…) and become a lifestyle resource as well as a real estate expert. This level of service will set you apart.

- Create a relevant Blog or make comments on the Blogs of others. Social networking on sites like Active Rain can also build your visibility in the business and with consumers.

Use targeted mailing lists

Media research evaluating how welcome unsolicited, direct response advertising is found that addressed (person's name as opposed to dear homeowner) direct mail is viewed as "most to fairly welcome" by 40% of recipients. Unaddressed marketing pieces drop to a 23% welcome level. Compare this to telemarketing with a 19% welcome rate. More surprising was the unwelcome reaction to unsolicited email, only 11% welcome the unexpected email in their inbox. Direct mail can be a valuable tool, but recognize it will be most effective when it is the right offer at the right time. Even targeted, direct mail remains somewhat of a numbers game.

If you are not sure about how to find consumer mailing lists, it's time to use your favorite Internet search engine again. Enter the description of the kind of list you'd like to have. For example, search for mailing list, affluent golfers or mailing list, plane owners. A variety of possibilities will be listed. You can go to the Websites for the best matches and quickly zero in on the list providers (usually called list houses or list brokers) who have what you are looking for. Compare prices, the list guarantee, and terms for the use of the list before you commit to renting or buying a list. Understand that most lists will be available for renting rather than for purchasing.

If you prefer, you can find lists by taking a trip to your library. Go to the business reference section. Ask the librarian for the Standard Rate and Data Service Direct Marketing Book. This book contains information on tens of thousands of business and consumer mailing lists. This book is most commonly used by advertising agencies and other marketing professionals. It may take you a quite while to decipher the abbreviations and marketing terminology, but it will be well worth the effort. If you have a friend in the advertising business who is willing to go along, he or she may be able to help shorten your learning curve. The book will help you identify specific consumer lists, list sources, and prices. It will also identify which lists are available with e-mail addresses and phone numbers. However, using your Internet search engine is probably a more efficient way to find lists.

You can also contact an advertising agency for list recommendations (look for an agency with specific direct mail expertise), but you will pay them a fee over and above the list rental fee. Individual list brokers (sometimes called list houses) can be found in the yellow pages in major markets. They can provide you with consumer mailing lists or what are called "b to c" lists. This stands for business (that's you) to consumers (potential prospects).

If you decide to rent a list, be sure you understand the terms of the rental. Lists are offered for a specific number of uses or for a set period of time. For instance, you may be able to use it only once or perhaps as often as you want for thirty days. Be sure you understand the conditions or terms for the lists that you rent.

Recognize that lists are "salted." That means they are lightly sprinkled with names of people who are not single millionaires who live in Florida and own boats; instead, they are people who work for the list house. Use the list in violation of the terms, and your phone will ring with a call from the list broker or you'll simply receive another bill for use of the list. If you are splitting a list with someone, be sure both your names are on the rental agreement.

You can create your own local mailing lists. Take the zip codes in your market and determine which ones are the highest income areas and have profiles matching the upper-tier buyer you are targeting. Sources for this information are available at the library in the business reference section. Look for the current year's copy of The Community Sourcebook of ZIP Code Demographics, published by ESRI. You can buy your own copy for about $500. Go to www.ESRI.com. The company publishes numerous sourcebooks; the zip code version is probably the best match for your needs. This publication has income, age, and lifestyle information for every U.S. zip code. Once you've spotted the zip code areas you wish to target, you can go to address/name directories to compile names and addresses of residents or you can rent relevant lists.

In addition to these geographic lists, keep past client and customer lists, and develop lists of local executives, business owners, or other affluent individuals. Computerize your databases and keep them current for easy use. As you develop your lists, be sure to add e-mail addresses and phone numbers whenever possible. Also add the zip plus four information since it will be required at some point by the U.S. postal system.

Author's Note: Institute members will find a good list source for affluent consumers in the member's only section of our Website.

Direct mail works if you do it properly

An often-quoted rule in advertising is Mayer's 40-40-20 rule of direct mail, which says that 40 percent of the success of your mailing is the quality of the list; 40 percent is your offer/product/service and credibility; and 20 percent is attributable to the creative aspects of the mail piece (the copy, graphics, format, use of color, etc.). The preceding section dealt with targeted mailing lists and how to find them, so let's turn to your offer/product/service and credibility. The offer/product/service will obviously vary depending upon whether your mailing is a property offering or a general prospecting piece. If you are mailing to past clients and customers or to a group that you have consistently (and effectively) farmed, you probably already have credibility. If you are mailing to a new group, you will need to focus on quickly establishing that credibility. The professional look and overall content of your mailing will help to do that as will the use of testimonials or success stories.

When it comes to the creative aspects of your direct mail, think quality. Use high quality paper, professional looking photographs, well written copy, and proof everything carefully to correct errors. An old trick of proofreaders is to read your copy through looking for errors, get someone else to read it, and then read the copy backwards word-by-word starting with the last word. It won't make sense, but you will catch spelling errors and double words as you focus on each word individually.

Here are a few suggestions to enhance the creative aspects of your mailing:

Always include a letter with a property brochure. Letters add importance and allow you to personalize the mailing. Think of a letter as a sales presentation. It should include a specific offer and invite the reader to take a specific action. For instance, "Call or e-mail me if you or someone you know would like to view this unique executive home" followed by your contact information. is a sales close or call to action. You'll want the body of the letter to be written to target the prospect as specifically as possible.

It's important to use a P.S. Advertising research tells us that the recipient of a letter first looks at the inside address and salutation, then looks to see who signed the letter, reads the P.S. and then decides whether or not to read the body of the letter. This is critical information to know when you are writing a sales letter. If the P.S. is more likely to be read than the letter itself, it makes sense always to include a P.S. and to use it to restate the key point in your letter, add another important point, or create curiosity that pulls the reader into the body of the letter.

Make your mailings YOU-oriented. As much as we might hate to admit it, we are all I-oriented. As a result, so are most letters -- even sales letters. Yet the most effective marketing letters are YOU-oriented. So, here's the challenge. Write your next sales or promotional letter. Then, go back though it and count the number of I/me/mine compared to you/your. Then rewrite the letter to minimize the I and maximize the YOU. This is harder than it sounds, but the result will be a much stronger, more effective letter.

Research says longer letters are better than shorter letters. If you've ever received the sweepstakes marketing letters from Publisher's Clearing House or the subscription offerings from Readers Digest, you know that their letters go on for pages and pages. Their letters are long because long, well-written sales letters work. If you review these professionally written, copy-tested letters you'll notice the use of headlines and subheads, underscored key points, multiple post scripts and other techniques to call attention to important information. This allows you, the reader, to skim through the letter and read the parts that are most relevant to you. Incidentally, this principle of longer copy being more effective also applies to brochure copy. A short paragraph and bullets points may be easy to write, but the result is an information piece, not a sales piece.

Here are two sample cover letters to go with brochures. Note the use of the P.S.

Date

Mr. Frank Jones
Success, Inc.
123 Entrepreneur Road
Kansas City, KS

Dear Mr. Jones:

Many business owners and professionals with whom I work put in long hours, work hard, and don't have much free time. As a result, they value their time at home and view their homes as private retreats. If you appreciate a home with lots of space, luxury, and comfort, you'll probably enjoy reviewing the enclosed brochure.

This wonderful home not only offers you a retreat from the pressures of work, it will make a statement about the success you've achieved. From the luxurious master bedroom suite to the unique home-entertainment theater and the convenient home gym, this home is exceptional. In the event that your business does demand your attention at home, you'll appreciate the 500-square-foot home office.

This property won't be on the market long. A successful individual will recognize its value and act quickly to enjoy its benefits. Could that person be you?

To take a closer look, please contact me for an appointment to tour this new listing. My phone numbers and e-mail address are on the brochure and on the enclosed business card.

Looking forward to hearing from you,

Sally Salespro

P.S. To see other exclusive property listings in our market and across the country, visit our Web site at www. com. I can also arrange for information or showings for any of the Internet properties in which you have an interest.

Headlines make non-personalized letters effective. If you do not have names to match some of your mailing addresses, resist the temptation to use a generic salutation. Dear Homeowner or Dear Neighbor is almost as much a turn-off as Dear Occupant. Instead, think of your letter as an advertisement directed to one person and replace the inside address with a headline and the salutation with a sub-headline. Using this approach, the inside address and salutation in the Dear Mr. Jones letter above might be replaced with the following:

Date

**Going home
can mean taking
a mini-vacation.**

It doesn't get any better than this.

Many business owners and professionals with whom I work put in long hours, work hard, and don't have...

Here's a brochure cover letter that combines both personalization and the headline concept.

Not for just anyone

**Desert retreat for a connoisseur
who has made his (or her) mark
and wants it all!**

Dear Mr. Smith,

If you're a spy for Interpol, corporate raider, reclusive celebrity, art maven, or just love the sight of the Arizona sun as it sinks behind the foothills, this house may send your excitement into the red zone.

Many will want it, but few will be successful enough to possess it. If $22 million is a comfortable investment for you, this home may be the one. In fact, don't even look at the attached brochure if you're not ready to experience desire.

This home was built as a labor of love. Not just designed, it was engineered, and built into the desert bedrock. It may well be this century's ultimate home – an icon for the 21st century, just as Frank Lloyd Wright's Fallingwater was representative of the 20th. The owner of this home will become a part of the history of American architecture. Architectural Digest has already come calling.

If you are a collector of the ultimate, treasure comfort and privacy, or want to be a "big dog" in an arts-oriented city, review the brochure, go to www.com, then contact me for a private showing.

My card is enclosed,

Sally Salespro

P.S. Did I mention this home has an Olympic gun range, a two-level gym, pool, wine cellar, and room for four stealth limos? (Ferraris or more ordinary cars will fit, too.)

Can you mail too much? More mail = better results. Chances are your mailings have multiple objectives. On one hand, you want to create visibility, position yourself as an expert in the upper-tier, and attract prospects. Another key objective is to sell your listings. How often do you have to mail to accomplish these goals? The answer is as often as possible. One approach is to schedule mailing much like sophisticated radio advertisers schedule ads -- in waves. Ads are run frequently during a short period of time, then stop for a short while, then run frequently again. The concept is that the "waves" of frequency create awareness, and the listener doesn't realize that the advertiser has not been on the air between the waves. In other words, you could mail for six weeks in a row, not mail for three, mail for six weeks, not mail for three, and so on. Continue that pattern and you will have created an impression that you mail almost every week without having to do so. If your mail pieces are well done, they will not be viewed as intrusive.

Junk mail is a matter of the wrong timing. Much of what you mail will be glanced at and thrown away because the timing of your offer wasn't right for the reader; however, if your name has registered one more time in the reader's mind, the mail was worthwhile. Your next mailing may catch the reader when he or she has a specific need. If so, you've built visibility and credibility with earlier mailings and increased the likelihood that the prospect will contact you. The timing of the offer is important.

Recently I was standing in my kitchen opening the day's mail. What I wasn't interested in was dropped into the trash compactor. I had just glanced at a catalogue, decided that it wasn't something I needed at that time, and started to throw it away. Before the catalogue landed in the compactor, my husband, who was walking past, scooped it up and said, "Oh, don't throw that away. I want to look at it." It was the Victoria's Secret lingerie catalogue. Because I wasn't in the market for lingerie that day, it was junk mail to me. The timing was wrong. For my husband, the timing is never wrong for that catalogue. It is never junk mail.

Telephone + Mail = Higher Response Rate. When direct mail is paired with a telephone call the effectiveness increases. To make the most of your direct mail farming, at least once a year, call the people on your mailing list on the day you mail to them and let them know to expect something in the mail from you. Since you are probably mailing to a large number of people, you might break your list into 12 groups and each month call the people in one of the groups. Follow do-not-call rules. Leaving a voice mail message will serve the purpose nicely. For example, if you send out a regular market update with statistics, you might call ahead and say, *"I've just compiled new data on what's happening in the luxury real estate market in our area. It's in the mail to you and should arrive in the next few days. If you have questions, please give me a call or send me an e-mail. If you, or someone you know, have real estate needs, I'd love the opportunity to help. In the meantime, I hope you find the market information interesting."*

If you are sending a just listed card you could call ahead and simply say, *"Today, I mailed a card to you announcing a new listing in our neighborhood. This is a wonderful opportunity to choose your new neighbors. If you have relatives or acquaintances who would like to live in the neighborhood, please pass the card along to them. And, of course, if I can help you with your real estate needs, please call."*

Ideas for mailing include:
An invitation to the Internet. People open greeting cards and invitations. So why not mail an invitation to visit your Website? If you have Websites for each of your luxury listings, you may want to do an invitation to those sites. Print it on nice invitation card stock and use an easy to read script typeface to address the envelope.

Sam Salespro
of
XYZ Real Estate Company
requests the pleasure of your company
on the Internet.

You're invited
to visit my Website
www.xyz.com
at your convenience
to review
fine home and estate property listings.

R.S.V.P. for information	**Sam Salesperson**
on any of our properties	**000-000-0000**
on the Internet	**sam@xyz.com**

Market Update Reports. Once you've gathered relevant statistical information about your local upper-tier market and the demographics of the local zip code areas you serve, keep it current and create a luxury home report. You can include the charts we've already talked about as well as some of the demographic information. Do this report on a regular basis and send it to your luxury farm areas, centers of influence, other types of professionals with whom you network, post it on your Webpage, and use it with your buyers and sellers.

A success story postcard. Highlight your expertise and service with a brief story outlining how you helped a prospect accomplish specific luxury home goals.

An impossible dream?

"We were looking for a wooded, water view property and we'd almost given up. Then, we met Sally. She had a property in mind, called the owner, and sure enough, she was able to bring the property onto the market. We wrote an offer immediately after seeing the house and had a signed contract within 12 hours. Now we can watch the ocean from our deck in the trees. Thank you, Sally!"

--Hillary and Bill Johnson

If you are interested in buying or selling, tell me your goals and I'll do my best to help you achieve them.

Call 000-000-0000 or e-mail me Sally@xyz.com.

--Sally Salespro

A testimonial postcard. Testimonials are almost as powerful as referrals. Collect them from satisfied buyers and sellers and use them in all your promotional materials. A postcard featuring testimonials is a strong credibility builder.

Sally Salespro's clients say, "It pays to work with a pro!"

"We were concerned about moving into a new city and finding a home where we could have horses. Sally gave us an overview tour, identified the equestrian communities, and then showed us the available homes. We chose the one we liked and Sally helped us negotiate the right price and coordinated a long-distance closing. With a buyers' agent like Sally, the real estate part of the move was easy.

--Eric and Cathy Welch

"When we were ready to build a new custom home, Sally helped us find the right builder and a fabulous 10-acre lot. She was masterful when it came to marketing our current home and helping us plan so that the settlement dates for both properties were perfectly coordinated for an easy move. When you work with Sally, you work with a pro."

--Olga and Vincent Hermann

Call the luxury home expert with YOUR real estate needs.
Sally Salespro 000-0000, E-mail Sally@xyz.com

Consistent, targeted direct mail works. Put it to work to help build your visibility and credibility.

CD or DVD marketing has impact

What you send through the mail doesn't have to be limited to traditional printed mail pieces. Sales and marketing professionals of all kinds are using presentations on CDs and DVDs.

The ability to target prospects has changed the faceless mass market of the past into audiences of one. The low cost of CD and DVD reproduction allows you put a powerful sales message into the hands of those prospects. When your prospect receives a CD or DVD they perceive that it has value.

Research by the Wharton School of Business at the University of Pennsylvania and reported in a special supplement to AdWeek magazine several years ago shows:

- 90% of those who receive a promotional video will watch it
- 85% will watch it on the day the video is received
- 94% are watched by more than one person
- 50% are watched more than once
- 89% are passed along to family or friends

The novelty of CDs and DVDs may have worn off a bit since this research, but nonetheless, a video message still has impact.

A video message offers many advantages. The combination of sight, sound, and motion is as powerful as television advertising but allows more time to deliver your message. The viewers also have control, they decide when and where to view the video and so, are at their most receptive when watching. A quality video entertains, informs, establishes a mood, creates a positive impression, and allows you to present your sales and benefits message in a dynamic, compelling way. The CD or DVD can also link prospects directly to your Website if watched on the computer. Online videos are a good option, too.

A video on CD or DVD can be a powerful tool to use to generate or close prospects. If your firm has a company video or a luxury home marketing system video, use it. Consider creating one with information about you, your firm, your approach to marketing luxury properties, and testimonials from your upper-tier buyers and sellers.

Institute member Laura Duggan, a partner of Sotheby's Capital City in Austin (TX) builds her property marketing plans around individual Websites for each of her upper-tier listings. She calls her Website-based approach her "Platinum Sales System." One integral part of her marketing is a three minute video (on CD) which Laura provides to prospective sellers in advance of her first appointment with them. The video talks about the marketing plan which Laura will implement and shows specific examples of the kind of Web based promotion she will do for the seller's home. This CD is delivered (not mailed) in beautiful packaging as part of Laura's pre-listing packet. Laura also has this video on her personal Website. One Austin seller who found it Online while looking at properties called her and said, Come list my home ($13.5 million!), you obviously know how to market properties." This is just one example of how an agent has used video marketing successfully.

Author's Note: Laura has had such success with her Platinum Sales System that we've asked her to make it available to our members so they have templates for easy and complete property

Website creation, their own customized video, and more. Find more information on our Website.

The uses of CDs and DVDs are limited only by your imagination and your budget. For instance, if you list homes for a custom builder, you might produce a video that includes a brief interview with the builder, floor plans and renderings of the homes being built, photographs and tours of completed homes, testimonial quotes from satisfied buyers, and a link to the builder's Webpage and other relevant sites. To help fund the production and distribution, the builder might produce fewer brochures (use the video piece instead) and place fewer printed mass-market ads. The video can also be available on your Website and on the builder's site.

National vendors such as Realty Video USA and Inman Stories produce short, quality videos for promoting luxury properties or other marketing purposes. Sometimes local TV stations will do affordable video production work. If you have a college or university in your area, contact the school to see which departments offer advertising, television production, or other courses attracting talented students. Talk to the professors about structuring a special project. For instance, start discussions by proposing that students work on your video for class credit and you cover direct expenses.

E-mail can be effective, too

Increasingly, successful agents are turning to e-mail in addition to traditional mailings. The speed and savings which e-mail generates make it a very desirable marketing tool. Most of the basics for effective direct mail can also be applied to e-mail communications. The stronger your connection with recipients and the more relevant they view the communication to be, the more likely your email will be read. With the glut of spam, email recipients are looking first to see who sent this email. Then asking themselves what's my relationship with the sender, even before looking at the subject line. Over doing your email can cause the consumer to hit the delete command each time they see something from you. Ask yourself if the communication is really relevant to the recipient. If not, don't send it. Strive to get maximum benefit from fewer emails.

Begin collecting e-mail addresses for your past clients and customers and for your farm areas and centers of influence. Why not do a special mailing to collect e-mail addresses and to confirm prospects' interest in receiving e-mail from you? This opt-in approach allows your e-mails to be distinguished from unwanted junk e-mail or spam. The card below should get you started. You might also add this note to your open house sign-in sheets and other communications with prospects.

The Real Estate Market is Changing!

**Please share your e-mail address with me
so I can share current market updates
about home sales and prices in your neighborhood
with you...**

**Just e-mail your address to me at
Salespro@XYZRealty.com
Then watch for regular Market Updates.
Call me if I can assist with your real estate needs
Sally Salespro
000-000-0000**

As you have probably already discovered, e-mail offers tremendous advantages. It is delivered immediately and costs less than traditional mail. E-mail marketing offers you the ability to add visual interest to your communications. Most of the direct mail ideas already discussed in this chapter can be adapted from snail mail to e-mail.

You can also create e-mail that, with a simple click, will send prospects to your Webpage via a hyperlink. Have your Webpage designer help you set up "landing pages" on your site. These are the pages where the user will land when clicking the hyperlink. The content of this landing page should relate to the message you have sent. For instance a message about the monthly activity in the upper-tier market should click to the full report on your Website, bypassing your homepage. A new listing message should click to your Online brochure for the new listing. You may also want to ask your Webpage designer to set up tracking reports for you. This is usually done by inserting a few lines of HTML code on the pages of your Website so that the number of respondents can be measured. Over time, this will allow you to evaluate the types of e-mail messages that are most effective for driving people to your Webpage.

HTML-formatted e-mail newsletters are offered by vendors in many markets. These newsletters are personalized for individual agents, have content specific to a market area, and look like sophisticated WebPages. Because these newsletters contain color graphics, photographs, and special type treatments, they may have more impact than all-text e-mail messages. In many cases, e-mail newsletters will be sent out automatically for you if you upload your contact address list to the vendor. These newsletters will not be targeted specifically to the upper-tier, so be sure the content is appropriate. Newsletters that you purchase do not replace your own market updates for the upper-tier; they are a supplementary marketing tool.

The Internet should be an important part of your strategy

Leslie Appleton-Young, the chief economist and vice president of the California Association of Realtors® (CAR) keeps her finger on the pulse of the Internet and its use in real estate. According to CAR research she coordinated in 2006, 70% of homebuyers surveyed reported using the Internet as an important part of their home-buying and selection process. Compare this to 2000, when only 28% did. Of these Internet buyers, 92% found their agent on a Web site, 63% through an Internet search engine. Not one of the Internet buyers found their agent through brochures, flyers, yard signs or mailers to their home.

What is even more telling, 100% of buyers surveyed started looking at homes first, agents second. When you add that to the fact that 81% of Internet buyers stay with the first real estate agent they contact, you'll understand the importance of the Internet in your prospecting.

Compared to traditional buyers, Internet buyers spend more time researching properties online before actually looking at homes, look for a shorter time, view fewer homes, prefer to communicate via email and are more satisfied with their agents. In short, they are desirable buyers to have.

The affluent tend to be early adopters and they are Internet savvy. The $200,000 plus annual income group spends an average of 18 hours per week on line. The Web is one key place to connect with wealthy prospects. You need to give time and attention to harnessing the Web as a marketing tool.

Effective Internet strategies, Webpage design, how to maximize your email marketing, to blog or not to blog, are very specialized topics. Turn to the experts in Online marketing and build your knowledge and skills in this critical area. The good news is there are lots of resources to help you. Here are just three quick suggestions (two books and one networking organization) to get you started.

- *Real Estate Rainmaker Guide to Online Marketing*, by Dan Gooder Richard, John Wiley and Sons publisher
- *Realty Blogging: Build Your Brand and Outsmart Your Competition*, by Richard Nacht and Paul Chaney, McGraw-Hill publisher.
- Allen Hainge's Cyberstars group, information at www. afhseminars.com

Educating prospects can point them to you

Create an information/sales piece that will help you explain to a prospect why it makes sense to select an agent (like you) who specializes in the luxury market. The sample below is designed to be used as a part of your marketing consultation or in the initial interaction with your buyer prospects. Its objective is to help you get the business by reinforcing important criteria for selecting a luxury home expert. For a downloadable PDF copy that you can print or post Online, visit the member only section of www.LuxuryHomeMarketing.com. (Be sure to read it before you use it so you can present yourself as meeting the suggested criteria.) You may want to include it in your pre-listing materials and use it in your other marketing as appropriate.

If you are not an Institute member, use the sample below as an idea generator for creating your own checklist. If you change the sample, just be sure to remove the author credit.

**Five tips for selecting
the right real estate professional
to help you buy or sell your luxury home**

Laurie Moore-Moore
Founder
The Institute for Luxury Home Marketing

Not all good agents operate effectively in the upper-tier market. It is a market segment which requires special competencies. Here are some general guidelines for choosing an agent to assist you in the upper-tier residential marketplace.

1. Look for market knowledge and real estate skills. Not only should your agent know the city or area you are interested in, he or she should be knowledgeable about the price range you've targeted. A luxury home expert should be able to discuss the amount of inventory available, the average number of days a property is on the market before going under contract, the number of sales in the last 30/60/90 days, and the list to sale price ratio – all by price range. The more knowledgeable the agent is about the upper-tier market, the more valuable he or she can be as a resource for you. When you schedule your first meeting with a prospective agent let the agent know you want an overview of the market conditions based on your price range. A solid track record of success is a clear indicator of market savvy. Don't choose an agent based on country club membership, the kind of car he or she drives, or similar criteria. Do choose your agent based on the answer to this question: "Does this agent have the competencies necessary to help me accomplish my real estate goals?"

2. Notice special designations and ask what they mean. Some real estate professionals have earned their broker's license which means they have had additional training and a certain amount of experience. You'll also find agents with designations based on education and experience such as "Certified Luxury Home Marketing Specialist." These credentials add credibility and reflect actual market performance. This doesn't mean that you should ignore a newer agent without designations. A bright, creative newcomer who's willing to work hard, do the market research, and has targeted the upper-tier can often provide excellent service, too.

3. If you are selling, ask that the listing presentation include a specific marketing plan for your property. In fact, if your agent calls this meeting "a marketing consultation appointment" rather than listing presentation, that's a good sign! Don't assume that the best marketing plan is always the most expensive. Listen to why the agent has included each element of the plan. Your agent should outline the complete plan and explain it. Look at the quality of the marketing pieces the agent has used in the past as part of your evaluation process. If the home is very, very expensive or the buyer is likely to come from outside the country, your marketing plan will need to be especially creative. Networking with other luxury home sales professionals should always be an important aspect of the marketing plan.

4. If you are selling, don't let an agent "buy" your business. Choosing a real estate professional based on the highest suggested list price is counter productive if the house is overpriced. The agent doesn't set the price – the marketplace does. If your home goes on the market as an overpriced listing, agents and their prospects will quickly move on to other properties which offer more value relative to cost. Will they come back if the price goes down? In many cases, no.

5. Rapport and clear communication are important. Buying and selling can be stressful. Choosing an agent with whom you communicate clearly and easily will help simplify the process. Be sure he or she understands your needs and expectations and that you understand the process and the agent's expectations of you.

In short, specialized knowledge + quality tools + clear communication = real estate professional who can deliver the results you want in the luxury home arena.

BONUS TIP: If you have an agent with whom you've successfully worked with in the past and now you are looking in a new part of the country or different corner of the world, ask that agent to refer you to a luxury home specialist in the new locale. Upper-tier agents network, often attend national or international meetings, and many have earned special professional designations and have contacts with others with the same credentials. Good agents know their own credibility is on the line when they refer and will carefully pre-qualify another real estate professional before referring.

© Laurie Moore-Moore, Institute for Luxury Home Marketing, Dallas (TX), 2002, revised 2007

Selling a country club lifestyle?
Club membership directors can help you
(No, you don't have to be a member)

Luxury homebuyers are often excellent prospects for country

club memberships as well. To enhance your selling ability and your service to your prospects, target clubs in the area where you work and get to know the club membership directors.

When you have a prospect looking at homes in the club area (especially out-of-towners), utilize the membership director as a resource. This is especially effective for prospects who are looking for a country club lifestyle as part of their luxury home purchase. You don't have to be a country club member to network with the clubs in your area. Membership directors appreciate the opportunity to show their facilities to qualified member prospects, and your clients will appreciate your helping them find a club that matches their needs.

Membership directors can be sale enhancers by helping you sell the area lifestyle. They can help reinforce buying decisions and be excellent sources of buyer and seller leads. Club membership directors can be valuable networking partners. What's more, networking is easy. Contact the membership director when you have prospects interested in a country club community.

Ask the membership director to:

Schedule lunch at the club for your prospects so they can get to know the club and its facilities. When you are showing buyer prospects but need to juggle other tasks, line up some additional properties to show, or just make some phone calls. Being able to drop off your prospects for lunch at the club not only allows them to familiarize themselves with the club and meet the membership director – who will help you sell the area or reinforce a buying decision that's about to be made – it also frees you for an hour or two to take care of business. Generally the club will provide a complimentary lunch and club tour for your prospects and will usually do it on short notice.

Match prospects with members for golf, tennis, or other activities. If your prospects are looking for a country club lifestyle, membership directors will often agree to schedule tennis or a round of golf for your prospects to help them evaluate a club. They'll team your customers up with existing members who can be counted on to extol the benefits of the community and the club. This allows prospects to identify the clubs that are the best matches for them. At the same time, it demonstrates the added value service you offer.

Cooperate with you on a welcome or closing gift. Often they'll bear the cost and enclose your card as well as that of the membership director. Clubs will often provide gifts for you to present to your upper-tier buyers (these are also tools for selling club memberships). Sample gifts might include a complimentary dinner at the club following property purchase, moving day picnic baskets, or congratulations cakes prepared by the club's kitchen.

Refer business to you. Ask the club's membership director for buyer and seller referrals. Some people shop for country clubs before they shop for homes. The membership director is also often aware of members who are planning to leave the area. Not only can you help these homeowners sell, you can also refer them to their new locations. Provide your business cards to the membership director and ask him or her to suggest you and hand out your cards when coming across buyer or seller prospects. If you are able to get a club membership list, add it to your center of influence and farm the list.

Provide information about the club that you can add to your relocation packets, use to enhance your Website, and use to help position you as the country club community expert. Add information about the clubs in your area to the community relocation packets you send to out-of-towners. Include club information in special information books you create for your upper-tier listings and add club information to your Website.

If you are in an area with multiple clubs, research the clubs and create a comparison chart to help match customers with the facilities in which they are most interested. After all, different facilities relate to different lifestyles. Develop a checklist of questions, do research, and then create a club comparison checklist or matrix. Posting this on your Website provides easy access to the information for prospects.

Questions you might ask about the club:

- What one-time and annual or monthly fees are charged?
- What dining facilities does the club have?
- What sports are available? (Golf, tennis, swimming, handball, squash, etc.)
- What pro and shop services are available?
- Does the club have a junior program for children?
- What member tournaments are scheduled for the various sports?
- When is the club not available for member sports (special tournaments, etc)?
- What other services are available (spa services, child care, etc.)?
- What is the dress code?
- How many members are there?
- What other clubs offer reciprocal privileges?
- If the club is in a club community, does a homeowner have

priority over a non-resident for membership? Priority for tee times?

- If a homeowner sells, can he or she transfer membership to the new homebuyer?

To enhance your position as an expert in luxury home properties, consider becoming an expert in the country club lifestyle options available in your community and start by networking with club membership directors.

Author's Note: These same concepts can be modified for tennis or racquet clubs, dining clubs, yachting clubs, equestrian centers, fitness centers and other facilities.

Add business owners, executives and professionals to your center of influence

Since the majority of very affluent fall into three occupation categories – entrepreneurs, corporate executives, and professionals – it makes sense to target these occupation groups. The following idea is one way to identify these individuals, target them and perhaps turn a cold contact into a warm lead.

Watch for business success stories. Everyone appreciates being recognized for his or her successes. Watch your local newspaper's business section, local and regional business magazines, and national business publications for business success stories. If you read about a local firm that wins a quality service award, a company that makes a major acquisition, a firm that goes public, a company that wins a big contract, an executive who earns a major promotion, or a lawyer who makes partner, clip out the article. Mount it on a piece of letterhead or other paper. You may need both sides of the sheet or maybe even two sheets.

Leave room to paste your business card on as well. Take this to your local printer, office supply or teachers supply store and have it laminated. Mail the laminated article with a note and a second business card to the business owner, relevant executive, or professional. Your note might say something like...

Congratulations on your latest business success.
If you're interested in moving up residentially as well,
I'd be delighted to show you some of the wonderful properties
available in today's market. Please contact me if you
or someone you know needs real estate assistance.
My card is enclosed. Again, congratulations.

The fact that the clipping you send is laminated increases the probability that the recipient will keep it. Since your card is laminated with the clipping, your name remains with the prospect, too. Enclose a second card inside the note you write. Add this executive to your "center of influence," the list of individuals to whom you send just listed/just sold or other luxury home farming mailings.

When you or someone in your office lists a luxury home, send the property brochure with another note and card with all your contact information. You might reference the original success again. For instance...

Your phone is probably still ringing with congratulatory calls
about your new government contract. When you are ready to take a
break from all that's involved in implementing your new contract, I
thought you'd enjoy reviewing this brochure about a simply charm-
ing English Tudor estate property that we have just listed. If you or
someone you know would like to see it, I'd be delighted to arrange it.
Just e-mail or call me.

After this executive has received several mailings from you, you may wish to initiate a phone contact to introduce yourself and ask if he or she would like to continue to receive property brochures by mail or if e-mail would be preferred. Also ask if there are specific real estate needs you might assist with. Remember to also ask for referrals.

In most cases the business phone number is what is most easily located. You will probably reach an assistant or secretary when you call. If the staff person is hesitant to put you through and asks the purpose of your call, your phone script might sound like this:

> *This is Sam Salespro with ABC Realty. I've been sending Mr. Smith printed brochures of some of our outstanding executive homes. Many of my other executive clients have asked me to e-mail them the brochures rather than mailing them. I just wanted to check with Mr. Smith and see if he'd prefer the PDF version also. May I speak with him, please?*

Decide in advance of calling whether you will use a first name or the more formal Mr. or Ms. The age of the person you are calling, the standard practice in your market, and what makes you most comfortable will all be part of your decision.

Be a resource for companies that are hiring from outside the area. If you are in a large market, get to know the headhunters who work at the executive level. Offer your ability to sell the community as a resource in recruiting. Often a prospective executive will want to know more about the community and perhaps even take an overview tour before accepting a job. If you are willing to make a call to answer questions about the area, send a relocation packet of materials, and perhaps conduct an overview tour, you may be rewarded with qualified buyer prospects.

Watch for companies advertising for executive level employees on their Websites or in regional or national media. Many firms advertise for executive job candidates in the national or regional editions of the Wall Street Journal. If you have a firm name, call and simply ask for the name of the vice president of human resources or top executive overseeing staffing, confirm the spelling of the name and the correct address. Then send a letter offering to help them recruit executive level staff by helping the company sell the area. This "you sell the job, I'll sell the area" approach can also result in business for you.

Be sure to position yourself as specializing only in executive relocations, otherwise you may find yourself looking for rentals for summer interns. If you have a relocation department or business development division in your firm, a corporate caller may already be offering these services to local companies. If so, talk with relocation about how you can earn the right to some of these referrals or take your leads to them and let them help you build the corporate relationships. Clarify up front what referral policies will apply. Even if you have to pay fees on some of the business, your center of influence with executive prospects will expand and your non-referral fee business will grow significantly over time.

Network with others who interact with the wealthy

Earlier in this book I suggested being a referral resource for services and products that the affluent need and networking with those sources. This advice can be expanded from country club membership directors (as discussed above) to include others who interact with the affluent. Teachers at private schools are often among the first to know that a family is relocating because the children announce it to their friends at school. Sales people for high end boats, marina and private airport managers, wine merchants, exclusive jewelers, interior decorators, private caterers, golf pros, riding instructors, and tennis pros all belong on your networking list. CPAs, executive headhunters, private bankers, stockbrokers, financial advisors, insurance salesmen, business brokers, are sources of executive contacts. The importance of networking can't be overemphasized.

Look for win-win opportunities in your networking. For instance, if you work in a waterfront area, network with high-ticket boat salesmen. Occasionally you might offer to enclose a brochure for an expensive boat with a property brochure mailing. Add a creative cover letter and perhaps you'll spark prospects' interest in boat and house. At the very least, you are highlighting the waterfront lifestyle you are selling and creating an opportunity for the boat seller to promote your listings. You might even ask the salesman to moor the boat in the home's boat slip during the photography session for the property brochure.

The cover letter for your house-and-boat mailing might start out with something like,

If you've dreamed of living in a beautiful four bedroom home on the bay with the opportunity to step out your back door and take a romantic midnight sail, this home is for you.

In the letter's post script or in the brochure you might say,

If you aren't already enjoying a boating lifestyle, look no further. The gorgeous 60 foot sailboat pictured in the boat slip is available from John Jones at ABC Yacht Sales. Prefer a powerboat? John has those, too. Your dream house, plus a dream boat – life doesn't get much better. You deserve it. Call us.

Think of other ways to work together. Schedule a joint broker open house and boat tour event with the boat salesman. Both house and boat will benefit from the exposure. Schedule a VIP open event in conjunction with a big boat show and invite your center of influence, your seller's list of friends and acquaintances, and the yacht company's client and prospect list. As you begin to network, many interesting cross-promotional opportunities will appear.

One of the more interesting networking strategies I've encountered is an agent who lives in a city with a number of gated neighborhoods with gate guards. She networks with the gate guards. When you think about it, it makes sense. She says that people will pull up to the gate and ask if there are properties for sale. The gate guard will tell them that unfortunately, he can't let them in but will then give them the agent's card and indicate that she specializes in gated communities and would be happy to show them what's available in this community as well as other gated communities. The agent keeps the gate guards happy with cookies and other goodies left over from open houses and occasional pizza delivery. She told me she closes millions of dollars worth of business each year as a result of gate guard referrals.

Work the custom builder market

Call on luxury homebuilders. Often smaller firms build just a few homes each year and don't have sales staff on site. If you can't convince them to list with you, ask them to refer you to their buyers who have homes to sell. If you are just getting started, you may even want to offer to hold a weekend open house for a builder's new home, or advertise a builder's home to capture calls from prospects. Be sure to include builders on your list when you mail your market updates. Joining your local chapter of the National Association of Home Builders is a good way to network and build your visibility in the new homes market.

Preview builders' spec homes, they are an important part of market inventory and may even be good comparables for properties you are pricing. Keeping up with the market's new construction will help you stay on top of current building and design trends as well.

A very successful agent in Los Angeles helped build her business by volunteering to hold open houses for builders' custom homes. Today she does over a hundred million dollars worth of business each year and her client list reads like a Hollywood who's who.

Chapter Eleven

Working with Rich Buyers

Pre-qualifying buyer prospects:
Are these folks for real?

In some situations, sellers may require that a prospect's ability to purchase be confirmed before a showing appointment is even scheduled. (Celebrities and others concerned about security may insist upon pre-qualification to help weed out curious sightseers.) This can sometimes be solved by having prospects pre-approved for their mortgage. If time precludes this or if prospects plan to be cash buyers, a letter from a private banker, brokerage firm or other financial entity confirming assets or credit available is another common way of handling the issue.

Pre-qualifying your buyer prospect is important regardless of price range. Don't jump to conclusions about an individual's ability to buy based on the car they drive or how they dress. A simple question to start the qualification process is, "How will you prefer to pay for the home you are considering buying?" One Institute member starts her prequalifying with, "Do you prefer to pay all cash for the home you'll be buying?" She says her prospects seem to love the fact that she believes they might be able to pay all cash.

However you choose to start the conversation, don't be hesitant to ask how they plan to pay. If they indicate that they will want a mortgage loan, offer to introduce them to a mortgage loan originator who can qualify them. If they indicate they have their own lending source, encourage them to initiate the approval process as quickly as possible. If they say, "We'll be paying all cash," that's terrific, but you still must prequalify them.

Develop scripts to help you ask for financial information. For instance,

For those who wish to purchase with a loan: *As you can understand, many sellers of luxury properties require that only pre-qualified prospects be given access to their homes. To ensure that I can show you the homes that you'll want—and need —to see before making a smart buying decision, and to maximize your negotiation power, we'll need to quickly get you pre-approved for a loan.*

For those planning to buy with cash: *As you can understand, many sellers of luxury properties require that only pre-qualified prospects be given access to their homes. To ensure that I can show you the homes that you'll want—and need —to see before making a smart buying decision, and to maximize your negotiation power, we'll simply need to have your banker, broker, or other financial institution provide a standard letter of financial introduction which verifies that you have the necessary assets to purchase in the price range in which you are interested.*

Be sure you have a system for requesting and collecting written asset verification information. You may want to develop a standard form or letter which your prospect signs granting a financial entity permission to give you information indicating that your prospect has assets sufficient to purchase at a particular price point. When this document is returned to you, be sure to pick up the telephone and call the individual who has signed it and confirm your receipt of the document. This is not just a courtesy, it is a critically important double-check that the document is real. If, when you call the financial institution's number on the letterhead, Tony's Pizzeria answers, you know you have a problem! Unfortunately, the upper-tier is plagued with scam artists who are not wealthy buyers even though they try to look and act the part. You don't want to put your sellers at risk or waste your time with them.

Some agents take the prequalifying of cash buyers a step farther. Once an all cash contract has been negotiated, a date prior-to-closing is agreed upon for the buyer to deposit the cash into an escrow account at the title company (or other appropriate place).

While the qualifying approach above is standard in the upper tier, industry speaker and author Michael Merin has a slightly different opinion and suggests that having cash buyers pre-approved for a loan (whether they plan to use it or not) may be an even better strategy.

Merin suggests having all affluent buyer prospects pre-approved in his training sessions for experienced agents. Invariably, he says a nicely manicured hand is raised and the agent explains that in her market, agents would never think of asking their wealthy buyers about their finances. It just isn't done

It should be done, Merin emphasizes. "If an agent is asking some buyers whether a lender has pre-qualified them in the last 60 days and is not asking others, the agent is violating fair housing laws by treating potential clients differently.

"Asking the question may also set the stage for more effective negotiation for your home buying client," Merin adds. "Your buyer may chuckle and reply that money will not be a problem and refer you to a broker, or private banker for a verification of assets. However, simply including this letter with your offer can send a red flag right up the pole announcing your prospect's wealth." Instead, Merin suggests you should urge your wealthy buyer to become pre-approved for a loan. "In my experience, rich buyers often have a friend or close acquaintance who owns their own bank and can easily have a legitimate pre-approval letter prepared.

"While ability to pay and willingness to pay are two different issues," says Merin, "few sellers will reduce their asking prices for your buyer clients when the sellers learn the buyers are rich. This is not just a cash buyer, the seller will conclude, but a wealthy client."

In some states, agency laws and regulations allow you to write the offer and keep the buyer's identity anonymous. This can work if it is a common practice, but beware of falling into the same trap. To the extent that it is common for only wealthy buyers to submit offers anonymously, you may raise that same flag announcing the wealth of the potential buyer.

Merin also believes that almost as important as convincing the buyer to become pre-approved, is advising the buyer to work with the right lender — someone who will satisfy the listing agent's questions without revealing too much. "When called by the listing agent," Merin suggests, "the lender should answer that the ratios or credit scores are acceptable and the buyer's cash reserves are sufficient rather than revealing what the front-end and back-end ratios are, what the credit score is, or how much money the buyers have available. A pre-approval commitment (not just a pre-qualification letter) with the right lender is a powerful negotiating tool."

Unless you are a tax accountant, leave the discussion of the tax implications of a purchase to the experts. As you work in the upper-tier, you will develop relationships with experts in real estate related fields. If your affluent clients need specialized assistance, you can refer them to knowledgeable practitioners who hopefully will reciprocate by referring their clients with real estate needs to you.

While you may diligently prequalify your buyers, not every agent will be as conscientious. This raises the question of how to handle showing requests for prospects who have not been prequalified by their agents. Your seller (with your input) should to decide whether or not to allow these showings. Some sellers will be adamant about prequalification, others less so. One approach is to suggest to your seller that if the agent making the request is someone you believe to be a knowledgeable luxury agent, the showing be allowed. But, it should be treated as an agent preview until you know the prospect is qualified. The advantage of this is that the agent will subsequently have your listing "top of mind" and think of it for his or her next qualified buyer. The negative is that you don't really know the prospect's true motivation for wanting to see the house.

Showing buyer prospects

The basic principles for showing a home are same regardless of price, but recognize that busy, affluent buyers may have no patience for agents who haven't previewed homes before showing them. Be certain the homes meet the condition requirements of the buyer and that they are consistent with what the buyer is looking for — just being in the right price range isn't enough. You are selling amenities, quality of finish, location and lifestyle, not just square footage. If you feel that a buyer needs to see a home that may not meet their exact criteria but has other features that you think make it a viable option for the prospect, be sure you explain up front. Otherwise they'll think you aren't listening.

It is important to note that in some markets, very expensive properties may have sellers who ask that the listing agent be present at every showing. In this case, the listing agent may even assume the responsibility for showing the home and all of its special amenities.

If you are pursuing a listing in a market where accompanied showings (listing agent must be present to show) are common, recognize that this will require extra time and commitment on your part. If you plan to have your assistant help with this, be sure you know your state's requirements regarding appropriate tasks and licensing for assistants.

Florida agent Wayne Adams (who works the Tampa Bay luxury home market with his wife Joyce, who is also his business partner) prefers to handle the showings of their listings and understands how to sell in the process. Recently he and Joyce listed a million-dollar waterfront home. Another agent called to schedule a showing, telling Wayne that the prospects had looked at 50 homes over a year's time and were satisfied with none of them. After many questions from Wayne about what the buyers liked and disliked, the showing was confirmed for later in the day.

When the agent arrived with buyers in tow, Wayne took them into the foyer and said, "I understand that you have looked at 50 homes during the past year. This is the last one you need to see because..." The next two minutes were spent with Wayne outlining how this home had everything they liked with none of the features they disliked.

When Wayne finished, the husband said, "Wayne, you are aggressive."

Wayne's laughing answer was, "I haven't been called that low key in years."

After orienting them to the home, Wayne guided the prospects through the property pointing out the details that supported his conversation in the foyer. Within 10 feet of the door, the wife said, "This is nice." A little later the husband commented, "This is good value for the money." (Buying signs!) The next morning, the buyers' agent faxed a cash offer for almost full price with just an inspection contingency. The property closed in two weeks.

Wayne is right when he says that bringing qualified buyers to the door is just the first step in a successful marketing program for a listing. A second major step is a having a showing and selling plan once they are in the home. This assumes that you have done some information gathering about what the prospect's priorities are and what likes and dislikes they've expressed when viewing other properties. Controlling the showings of your listings takes time but it actually gives you the opportunity to SELL the home to prospects by demonstrating how it meets their needs.

If the buyer is your prospect and you prefer to show the home yourself, be sure you have previewed the property and understand how to show it effectively.

Here's a perfect illustration of how to show someone else's listing: Institute member Debra King, of Diane Turton Realtors®, (NJ), "romanced a house" into a dream dwelling for her client and a million dollar plus sale for herself. Debra received an

Internet lead from a potential buyer for a unique home listed by another agent in her company. Deborah felt this home was a good match for the buyer prospect. "I'm going to sell this property!" she challenged herself, and promptly got to work. At an asking price of $1.9 million, the 6,700 square foot, non-waterfront property had already been on the market for nearly a year. From a prior visit, Debra knew the home's fabulous features were too numerous to grasp in a single viewing.

Two days before she was to show the home to the potential buyer, Debra toured the property with the owner, making copious notes of features such as limestone flooring, copper-infused slate, radiant heat, professional murals by a Russian artist, 12-foot double mahogany doors, beveled glass windows, and a movie/media room, among others.

That evening, using her notes and a list of features the owner had provided, Debra prepared a five-page brochure for the Floridian-style home, presenting the unique property room-by-room, accompanied by professional photographs. She memorized the details and the rooms in which they were located in order to romance the home as she presented it to potential buyers. On the day of the presentation, Debra did just that — to the degree that the potential buyers returned later that afternoon for a second visit, subsequently making an offer of $1.3 million, allowing for completion costs of the new construction.

Once an offer was made, a bidding war ensued on this property which had been on the market for months! Debra "romanced" the home repeatedly during the negotiations, always keeping her client focused on the prize. The property was eventually sold to her client for $1.4 million. Knowing exactly what her client was looking for in terms of size, style, and location enabled her to guide him in acquiring a dream home and lifestyle for his family.

Debra obviously understands the power of knowing your product and how to present it effectively. She wasn't the listing agent, but she took the time to do more than just preview the property. She understood her buyers wants and needs, studied the features and benefits of the house and decided how those related to the lifestyle her buyer prospect was looking for. Her "romancing" and effective showing of the house allowed the buyer to appreciate what it would be like to live there and as a result, the sale was made.

Chapter Twelve

Working with Rich Sellers

Questions to ask when setting the marketing consultation appointment

What's a marketing consultation? It what you are probably calling a listing presentation. But the problem with the term listing presentation is that many sellers already believe that all we do is list a property in MLS and then fall to our knees and pray that it sells. Why reinforce that idea when you do so much more? (Prayer may be part of your marketing plan, but it may be hard to justify your fee if that's all you propose to do, since sellers can do that for themselves.) Instead, change the terminology to reflect what this appointment should be all about – consulting with the seller regarding the pricing and marketing of their home. This has the added advantage of setting you apart in the market. If the seller says, "Marketing consultation appointment?" You can reply, "Yes, our meeting will be about the pricing strategy and marketing plan for your home." That sets you apart from the agent trying to "list" the home.

The initial information-gathering step for your presentation is important. When you're on the telephone setting up the appointment for the marketing consultation, think about some key questions in addition to the basic ones. For instance, the answers to the questions listed below are valuable to know before you visit the homeowner and begin the pricing and marketing process.

When was this house last on the market?
This will quickly identify expired listings and also help you pinpoint the last time the property changed hands so you can more easily research the last sales price.

Do you know which builder built your home?
Was your home architect-designed? If so, by whom?
The answers to these questions may have an impact on the value or provide a marketing hook.

Has the house had media coverage in the past?
Perhaps the home was a show home for a charity, was featured in a national home design magazine, or has important historical significance. You can do some quick research and go into the listing presentation with information that that will help you establish quick rapport and make you more knowledgeable about the property. The question regarding media coverage may also reveal disclosure issues. If something happened in the house that caused the media to report on it, then you can sensitively probe a bit and find out what happened.

What was it about this home that caused you to buy it or that you've especially enjoyed?
The answer to this question will often reveal the sellers' hot buttons. They will tell you about the home's features that they think are most important. These may be the same features the next buyer will find appealing. You may also get information about the neighborhood that will be useful in your marketing.

Is there anything else I should know about your home?

This is another Magic Question. You'll get a variety of interesting answers. Sellers may describe special features or improvements they believe will add value to a property – perhaps a new kitchen, which they anticipate will return more than they paid for it 12 months earlier. Forewarned is forearmed.

You may also get some surprising answers to this last question. An agent in Ohio told me a story about asking the magic question, "Is there anything else I should know about your home?" as she was setting up the appointment for a marketing consultation appointment. The seller on the other end of the phone line said, "Well, the house is haunted. We have a ghost; but don't worry, it's a friendly ghost." He went on to tell her a very charming and romantic ghost story that dated back to Civil War times.

The agent said, "That's a wonderful story. When I put your house on the market for you, would you be comfortable if I called the lifestyle editor of the local paper? With the ghost story you just told me, I think we could get some great publicity for the house. How would you feel about that, would you be comfortable?"

The seller thought it was a great idea and gave the agent the listing. The agent called the editor of the paper's lifestyle section who agreed that the story would make an interesting feature article. On a Sunday morning, the paper featured an article with photographs about the haunted house. The sellers were quoted, as was the real estate agent who was referred to as an expert in the marketing of historic and upper priced properties. This was great visibility for the house and for the agent. Also mentioned was the fact that the home would be open for the afternoon. The line to get in the open house went down the sidewalk, down the street, and around the corner. The agent and her numerous helpers had to count people as they let them in because they didn't want more than a certain number in that house at any one time. Not all those attending were qualified prospects. However, on Monday morning in offices, in elevators, and probably in kitchens with neighbors visiting, the conversations went like this, "Did you happen to see the article about the haunted house? Guess what, we went to see it." That kind of word-of-mouth sells properties. In fact, the house sold within a week of the article having appeared.

So ask the magic question, "Is there anything else you'd like me to know?" You'll discover more facts about the house, perhaps discover a disclosure issue, or you may find a marketing hook you can use.

Send information in advance

You have the appointment to discuss marketing the property. Now's the time to further position yourself as a true professional. Put together a pre-listing packet of information about you, your firm, and (if you have one) your special luxury home marketing program. Use a courier service or recruit a responsible neighborhood teenager to deliver it before your appointment. Have your delivery person carry a clipboard, hand the prospect the packet and have them sign for it. This reinforces the importance of the material.

Some of the national upper-tier marketing programs and some individual agents have video presentations on CD or DVD that introduce prospects to the agents' special approaches to marketing luxury properties. These information/sales presentations are excellent tools to use. A firm in the northeast boxes their luxury home program video with chocolates, gourmet coffee, and a couple of coffee mugs bearing the company logo. The box is gift wrapped and delivered to the prospect with a note from the agent inviting the prospects to sit down with a cup of coffee and some chocolates and view the movie. A pre-meeting package could also include your personal brochure, information about your firm, testimonial letters from happy sellers, and a current market update.

You may have a seller presentation video on your Website which you use as a pre-listing tool. This can be very effective as well.

One visit or two?

When working with unique custom homes, your marketing consultation presentation will require two visits, one to see the property and a second visit to present your market analysis and pricing recommendation. On your first visit, tour thoroughly. I know that you can blitz through a house in no time at all and get the information that you need. You do it every time you go on the tour of your office's new listings, right? Fifteen, twenty, thirty agents traipse through a new listing and if the owners are there, they are standing at the open door amazed that that many people can go through the house so quickly and come away with any information at all. But you can; that's your business.

Don't do that in the first visit of your marketing consultation. Let your seller lead you through the house, tell you the stories, point out the gourmet kitchen, talk about the antique paneling in the library, or describe other features while you take notes and establish rapport and credibility. As you tour, acknowledge the positive features and make note of the negatives.

Try to get the seller's pricing expectations on your first visit.

While you might ask, *"Oh by the way, what are your pricing expectations for this property?"* the seller usually turns this question around and responds with. "You're the expert; what do you think?"

At that point it may be tempting to give a ballpark figure. Resist. Don't even give a range, because what's going to happen? The seller will take the high point of the range, carve it in stone, and never let you forget it. Instead, you want to sidestep the issue of price until you are ready to discuss it. You probably already use a script along these lines, *"I would never do you the disservice of taking price lightly. It's just too important. I want to go back to the office, thoroughly review the comparable listings and sales, give this some serious thought, and when I come back tomorrow, we'll talk about my recommended list price. We'll also talk about the marketing plan for your property."*

Here's an indirect and surprisingly effective way of determining the seller's pricing expectations. *"As I begin my comparable research, is there a particular property sale you'd like me to pay special attention to?"* Chances are the seller has heard about a neighborhood sale which he is using as a benchmark for the value of his home. Of course, the seller believes his home is worth much more! Often this property sold for much less than the final sales price the seller heard through the neighborhood grapevine. What's more the home may not be a reasonable comparable. If you don't ask this question, you may go back to the office and do the best CMA in the history of the world, ignoring the property your seller has in mind because it isn't a good comparable sale. However, your seller will look at your perfect CMA and think that you missed the most important comparable. He still has the incorrect price in his mind and nothing you can say seems to change his attitude about price. You are mystified as to why he's being so unreasonable in the face of your CMA.

By asking the question, *"As I begin my comparable research, is there a particular property sale you'd like me to pay special attention to?"* you can go back to the office, determine the price the home really sold for, decide if it is a good comparable, come back with your recommended value, and then be prepared to discuss the sale your seller heard about. This allows you to overcome what may otherwise be a silent objection to your suggested list price.

Use luxury market data to educate your sellers

Now's the time to use the market data you've been tracking. Pull out the charts and graphs showing days on market, number of real buyers, etc. and review them with your sellers. It's important that that they understand the realities of the market. This also establishes you as a real estate professional with substantial market knowledge. Remember that the majority of the luxury home buyers and sellers are successful business people. They understand the value of "the numbers," track their own businesses with statistics, and expect you to have real estate market stats at your fingertips. From your standpoint, an educated seller is a more realistic seller.

CMAs and executive summaries

Finding comparable properties for unique, luxury residences can be difficult. Don't attempt to price an upper-tier custom property on the first visit unless you are very, very knowledgeable. Instead, note the property's condition, special characteristics, and amenities. Then, research comparable listings and sales and prepare a complete market analysis.

You CMA should be thorough. When possible, include photographs of the sold and current comparable properties and be prepared to discuss the features and amenities of each property.

Remember that many of the homeowners in the luxury price range are business owners, corporate executives, and other professionals. These individuals are quantitative, bottom-line-oriented, and busy. Why not prepare a thorough market analysis and then create a one-page executive summary that has a couple of sentences on each comparable, summarizes the market conditions in the relevant price ranges, and presents the recommended list price? The businessmen and women with whom you work are used to receiving their information in this form and will relate to it immediately. They can cut to the chase and then delve into the details.

SAMPLE

Price versus selling time

Take the time to explain the relationship between selling time and price to the seller. You might show them a price and selling time continuum and ask them to place themselves on the price and time line based on their priorities for the sale of their home.

Highest price_____◊_____Shortest Selling Time

Based on their objectives, where would they put themselves on the timeline?

The answer will give you insight into which is most important to them and help them understand that the highest price and shortest selling time are usually trade-offs. If you just ask which is more important, highest price or shortest selling time, they'll probably just say, "Both." Asking them to place themselves on the price and time line will give you a clearer understanding of their priority.

Differentiating yourself at the marketing consultation meeting

Remember that first impressions are very important. You must look professional and project confidence and professionalism. Don't wing it; be prepared. Then, to differentiate yourself and your marketing consultation presentation, you must sell three things:

Sell yourself and your competencies. Why are you the best agent for the job? How will your experience, training, market knowledge, pricing ability, contacts, enthusiasm, etc., help you accomplish their objectives? This is about why you can accomplish their real estate goals more than it is about you —be confident, but leave your ego at home. Work to establish rapport and trust.

Sell your company. Your firm is most likely a well-known company in your market; leverage this visibility and credibility. Talk about the company, its resources, advertising, relocation connections, size, and how these things work to help you assist them in marketing their home. If your firm is part of a national brand, referral network, or has a luxury home network affiliation, this is usually perceived by sellers as an advantage. Explain the benefits. If you your firm is new or you are a one-person operation, spend some time establishing credibility and outlining the benefits offered by your company.

Sell your marketing plan for the property. Luxury home sellers want to know exactly how you plan to market their homes. Saying "I'll promote your home" isn't enough. They want to know how, where, and when. How will you use the Internet in your property promotion? What sort of property brochure will you do? They want to know the details of what you propose to do. The most effective presentation of your plan is in writing.

Obviously, your recommended list price is an important aspect of your listing presentation. As has already been mentioned, pricing can be very difficult when dealing with custom homes because there are so few comparables. The more knowledgeable you are about the market, the better able you are to peg the selling price. Remember the value of a pre-appraisal.

When you work in the highest price ranges, homes are unique. This makes it very difficult to do a one-step marketing consultation presentation unless you are already very familiar with the property. As said earlier, expect to do a two-step presentation. The first visit will be to tour the property, the second visit will be to discuss your suggested list price and the proposed marketing plan.

Polish your presentation

Start with confidence. You only have a few seconds to make a first impression. Walk into your meeting with energy and a smile. Although you need to be very careful with cultural differences if you are working with an international clientele, in general, some good rules for successful interactions in a US or Canadian business transaction include: Look prospects in the eye. Shake hands firmly. Make sure you have the correct pronunciations of all names. Thank them for the opportunity to present your service and be prepared. If you do work with clients from a variety of cultural backgrounds, make an effort to learn what's appropriate in the context of their culture. A good book on the topic is *Kiss, Bow, or Shake Hands: How to Do Business in Sixty Countries*, by Morrison, Conaway and Borden. There are special editions of the book for Asia and for Europe.

Be prospect oriented. While it is important to establish your credibility, the focus of your presentation should be the prospects' needs, not all your past accomplishments. Ask questions about their goals and expectations and take time to listen. Also personalize the presentation for each seller and home. Be you-oriented, not I-oriented.

Respond to their needs. Be sure that you address the questions and concerns they express. Although a marketing consultation appointment is a presentation, it should also be a dialogue. You gather information from them and then explain how working with you will help them meet their needs.

Be organized but flexible. Know what you are going to say, stay focused, and don't waste the prospects' time. If the prospect appears ready to make a decision to list with you, close. You don't have to give your entire presentation every time. Keep going and you may talk yourself out of a listing.

Establish clear communication expectations. Ask, *"As I begin marketing your home, how would you like me to communicate with you, and how frequently?"* The answer gives you valuable insights into what they expect. Do they expect to hear from you weekly? Do they prefer that you phone or email a weekly report? This is important to know. To some extent, they will evaluate your service is based on how well you meet their communication expectations. So, you need to know what their expectations are. You may have a communication system in place, if so, explain it to them. For example, you may call your sellers every Monday night between 6:00 and 8:00. Share this with your sellers up front. They may say, "Gee, every Monday night from 6:00 to 8:00 we have dance lessons." You need to adjust your communication. Otherwise, you'll be leaving voice mail messages, and they'll be wondering why they never seem to hear from you.

Follow-up after the listing presentation

Ideally, the marketing consultation should culminate in the immediate listing of the property. You've worked to establish rapport with the sellers. You've toured the home, letting the sellers point out the property's special features. You've discussed how you can help meet their selling objectives and why you're the agent who can best assist them. You've dealt with the issue of price. The final step in the presentation is asking for the business. However, if you are one of several agents presenting, and the decision is not an immediate one, you'll need to follow up.

Before you leave the listing presentation, acknowledge the importance of their decision and reinforce why you are the right agent for the job. You'll want to develop your own scripts, but here's an idea to start with:

> *"Selling your property is a big decision, and I understand that you want to choose your agent carefully. All I ask is that when you sit down to make your choice that you remember four things –*
>
> *1. My enthusiasm about your property*
> *2. My commitment to do a good job for you*
> *3. The customized marketing plan that's ready for implementation,*
> *4. That I can put the power of an effective luxury home marketing program to work for you."*

Then follow up:

- Have a "thank you for the opportunity" note or letter delivered to the homeowner as soon as possible after your presentation.
- Reiterate the four reasons to choose you in your note.

Keep following up:

- Create a sense of urgency with a deadline: *"If I can begin marketing your home this week, we can just make the advertising deadline for the next issue of such-and-such publication. I've attached some suggested ad copy for your review and suggestions. Let's finalize the MLS paperwork and begin the marketing process."*

- Share a success story: *"Another of my luxury home properties just SOLD! 1234 Main St. sold for 98% of the list price. Let me put the power of my luxury marketing program to work getting your home sold."*

- Recognize that some of the same techniques you use to follow-up with sellers in other price ranges can be adapted to the upper-tier. Take what already works for you and tweak it.

Presentation tips from a pro

Institute member Jo Ellen Nash, broker/owner of Nash and Company in the Vail Valley of Colorado, has been a successful agent for 25 years. During that time, she has made many successful presentations. Here are her "Dos and Don'ts" for making yours more effective.

Listing Don'ts	Listing Do's
Don't do a Listing Presentation (all about you)	Do a Marketing Proposal (all about them, what you propose to do for them)
Don't ever say to a home seller, "I sell more homes" (aren't I great?)	Do say to a home seller, "I sell homes for more" (I can benefit you)
Don't ever talk about personal promotion	Do say "Many agents specialize in personal promotion, I specialize in property promotion, is that alright with you?"
Don't ever ask a home seller, "How are you going to select a company?"	Do get right to the proposal

Listing Don'ts	Listing Do's
Don't ever ask a home seller, "What are you looking for in an agent?" (They are not looking for anything in an agent; they are looking to sell their home.)	Do sell the clients on themselves and sell their property back to them.
Don't ever sell yourself.	Do justify your fee by success. (More than service, people want success. They want you to get the job done, so focus on your skills.)
Don't ever say, "We'll try it at that price."	Do say, "Let's develop a pricing strategy." (Be a consultant.)
Don't say "We need to lower the price."	Do say, "If we want to preserve your equity we need to reposition your home in the marketplace. We do not want to be chasing down the market."
Don't say, "Let's take a look at similar homes"	Do say, "Let's take a look at buyers' behavior in our marketplace."
When people ask, "How's the real estate market?" Don't say, "It's great" or "It's never been better" or "It's unbelievable" or "I need more listings".	Do say "Thanks for asking. We are in a very opportunistic time right now. The challenge is..." or "The advantage to Sellers is..." or "The advantage to buyers is..."
Don't ever tell a buyer or seller that you have an assistant.	Do say that you have an associate or partner.
Don't try to build or sell a real estate business.	Do build or sell a real estate practice.
Don't say that you work out of an office.	Do say that you work out of regional sales and marketing center.

Listing Don'ts	Listing Do's
Don't ever tell clients what you did before real estate, unless you were a doctor, lawyer, CPA, professional athlete, Olympic champion or academy award winner. (It is an apology for your past. Don't broadcast things that are irrelevant. No one cares what you did before real estate.)	Do say, "I have one last question. How soon would you like to have your beautiful home sold to the right buyer? Then let's get started!"
Don't ever close by saying, "I'd love to represent you." (This states the obvious and sounds like you are begging.)	Do remember these basic rules. Your competitor will praise what they have done. Be different. Instead of praising yourself, praise the property and your sellers relentlessly. **YOU WILL GET THE BUSINESS!**

Chapter Thirteen

Marketing Luxury Listings

Positioning the property

The first step in marketing a property is to define clearly what it is you are selling. You need to develop a positioning statement for the house—a brief summary statement of the key features and benefits offered by the home. You also need to include the negatives. Ask yourself why someone would buy this home. This positioning statement will be your springboard for developing your marketing strategy and for developing your marketing materials. The statement is NOT ad copy, it is a summary of the key points you need to think about as you write your copy. Here are four examples of positioning statements:

Contemporary Florida Home in Gated Golf Course Community
Room for big family, perfect for entertaining
Kitchen needs updating
Well located for Tampa, St. Petersburg, Clearwater, and Airports

Panoramic Waterfront views
Your own private beach and deep water boat dock
Huge rooms, high ceilings, all the amenities
Remote location

English Tudor design, new construction
Elegant five-bedroom on five wooded acres
Equestrian community
Top-rated school system
Competing with builder's new inventory

Manhattan concierge condominium with park views
Health club, rooftop pool, and theatre room
Two bedrooms, no maid's quarters, 24th Floor
Upper West side
Needs some updating

Setting the marketing budget

While one percent is often a number quoted when agents talk about a marketing budget for a luxury property, there is no magic formula. A key budgeting decision factor is the current market situation. If the market is hot, the property is very desirable, and the expected selling time is short, you may not need to advertise in publications with extended deadlines or order brochures with long production times. A fast-moving market generally requires a lower budget. Conversely, if extended and extensive marketing is anticipated, a more substantial budget will be necessary. Rather than using a formula to set the budget, the market conditions and the salability of the house should determine what you need to invest in marketing.

Remember that it is important to track the days-on-market by price range so that you have a clear idea about how long it is currently taking homes at a particular price point to sell. Before you commit to your marketing plan, be sure you have a listing term long enough to give you an adequate amount of marketing time. If homes in the $2 million dollar price range in your area are taking an average of 220 days to sell, a six-month listing is not a reasonable listing period. You'll want to ask for at least 12 months.

Steps for developing your marketing plan

After looking at a property and reviewing market conditions, you probably have an approximate marketing budget in mind. Set that number aside for a moment.

1. Take a blank sheet of paper and ask yourself, "If I could do anything I wanted to market this property, what would it be?" Allow yourself to be as creative as possible and list all the things that come to mind. Don't limit yourself to paid advertising and basic things like the broker open event. For instance, what about PR ideas?

2. Next, review your list and prioritize it by asking yourself, "If I could only do one thing on my list to sell this property, what would it be? If I could do two things? Three? . . . " Continue prioritizing until you have ranked all the items on your list. Make a new copy of your list with the marketing ideas listed in sequence as prioritized.

3. Now take each item on your list and calculate what it would cost to implement that idea. Keep a running total. At some point your total will equal the marketing budget you have in mind. Draw a line separating those ideas from the others. Everything above that line is your standard marketing plan. Take marketing ideas left on your list, and then ask yourself, "If I had one percent more as a fee, what additional things would I do?" Identify those things and draw another line. Everything above that line is your full fee plus one program. Then ask, "What would I do if I had another one percent?" Draw another line after identifying those items. Everything above that line is the full fee plus two program.

To summarize, you now have marketing ideas in a list, broken into three sub-lists or chunks. The first is your standard full fee marketing plan. The second chunk provides additional marketing activities for your full fee plus one percent plan, the third chunk creates your full fee plus two percent plan. You might call these your ruby, sapphire, diamond programs or your silver, gold and platinum marketing packages. This approach gives you the flexibility to offer three professional fee choices based on the level of marketing the seller chooses. You can also add "negotiating chips" or extra services to the three-tiered program. For instance you might pay for four decorator boards at the gold service level, but the seller pays at the silver level. During your presentation you might agree to pay for the boards as part of the silver program in return for a longer listing term.

Even more important, this technique is likely to generate a more creative and effective marketing plan than if you just listed the first few marketing ideas which occurred to you and then realized that you had already reached the reasonable budget maximum.

This approach to planning sets the stage for effectively handling the question: "This is an expensive property; you are going to cut your commission, aren't you?" Your answer might be, "Actually, I'm so glad you asked about the professional fee, because I am going to give you your choice! The marketing plan we have just looked at is my silver marketing plan. I can also show you my gold marketing plan and my platinum marketing plan. Then you can decide which plan best meets your needs and objectives."

This technique for developing a marketing plan also gives you a basic marketing plan (which you can afford to implement at the professional fee you have negotiated) plus a list of additional marketing ideas that you might implement at the seller's expense. When the seller reviews your marketing plan and asks, "Aren't there other things you can do to market my home?" You are prepared to say, "Yes, I have a list of a number of other 'extraordinary' marketing efforts we can implement and I will make a commitment to you. We can add the other 'extraordinary marketing' to our existing marketing plan. I will implement those marketing activities, and it will only cost you $XX." In some markets, agents negotiate receiving these additional marketing dollars upfront from the seller. These dollars may or may not be refundable to the seller at closing depending upon what is negotiated.

Jim Corbin of Illustrated Properties in Wellington (FL) frequently asks for and gets seller funded marketing dollars. Here's what Jim says about how he implements this idea with many of his multi-million dollar listings: "When negotiating the length of the listing term with a seller that is participating in the 'extraordinary marketing' expenses, I create a sliding scale tying their participation in advertising costs to the length of the listing. For instance, on a multimillion dollar property, the proposed marketing plan might include professional photography, special color brochures, ads in major luxury home magazines (like Unique Homes, duPont Registry, Pinnacle, Robb Report, Christie's Great Estates magazine). So, I offer the seller three options.

1. If the term of the listing is one-year, the seller pays 100% of the extraordinary advertising and marketing expenses up front, to be reimbursed at closing out of my professional fee.

2. For a two-year listing term, the seller advances 75% of the advertising and marketing budget up front, to be reimbursed at closing.

3. For a three-year listing term, 50% of the marketing costs will be paid up front, to be reimbursed at closing.

Every six months, the seller receives a statement from me documenting the costs and I also include copies of all the advertisements. This technique gives me a reasonable time to get the property sold. It also creates a Golden Handcuff. If the listing expires with the property unsold and the seller does not relist with me, there will be no reimbursement of marketing costs. Tying reimbursement to listing term increases my chances of renewing listings – something which can be particularly important if you believe your upper-tier market is beginning to soften or feel that a property is so unusual that it will require an extended marketing time."

Procedures!
A system for implementing your marketing plans

As soon as you list a luxury property, begin implementing your marketing plan.

- Take all the elements of your plan and break each into specific tasks. If you are doing a full-color property brochure, you might have these production tasks: decide on size, format, and quantity; develop theme; write copy; schedule photography; have client review the copy and photographs; coordinate layout with brochure company; approve final proof; confirm delivery date.

- Take your task list, assign deadline dates, and identify who's responsible (this may always be you).

- Next, create a property-marketing calendar and enter all the tasks on their deadline dates.

- Each day, as you make your to-do list, enter the tasks that will keep your marketing plan on track. Recognizing that this is a crazy business, you will often have days when you don't accomplish anything on your to-do list. Instead you are scrambling to hold a transaction together, working with a last-minute prospect, or preparing for a marketing consultation appointment. When that happens, you need to take the next available opportunity to catch up on your marketing plan tasks.

- When you have a few minutes, ask yourself what you need to do to get your marketing plan implementation back on schedule. Then do those tasks. If you don't deliver on your marketing as promised, you'll quickly find yourself out of business in the upper-tier market.

Set the Stage for a Sale

You're excited because the owner of a multi-million dollar home is ready to list with you. You're also a bit apprehensive. Despite the fact that the home is definitely upscale, you know you need to talk with the seller about staging the home to maximize its marketability and value. In other words, now's the time to have a conversation explaining that how one lives in a house and how one sells a house are different.

Staging can be as simple as fine tuning a well decorated luxury home to ensure it is spotlessly clean, uncluttered, and light and bright. At the other extreme, staging may require emptying the home and totally refurnishing and accessorizing it. If you have the time and an aptitude for decorating, you may choose to stage your listings yourself. If not, there are many staging services available. In either case, artful staging can shorten the selling time and increase the sales price.

Institute member, Jo Ellen Nash, of Jo Ellen Nash & Company, a successful luxury home broker serving the Vail Valley of

Colorado as well as Naples (FL), offers staging to her sellers. "We now have our own warehouse with model furnishings and accessories for staging listings that need a better market presence," says Nash. Her firm also has a company moving van to simplify the process. Nash acquired much of her furnishing inventory from builders closing their new home models. (Estate auctions, hotel auctions, consignment stores, and bankruptcy sales are other good sources of furniture and accessories for use in staging homes.)

According to Nash, staging increases marketability. "One of our listings had worn, contemporary furnishings, showing dismally. The listing had expired with another broker, so we assessed the property with a sharp eye. At our request, the seller removed the furnishings and re-carpeted. We furnished the home completely, down to the accessories, artwork and plants. Showing activity picked up immediately, with rave reviews from showing brokers. It quickly went under contract, with another contract in place!"

Most local markets have interior decorators who will consult with sellers, fine tune furniture and accessory placement, stage rooms for photography or special events, even totally redo a home with rented furnishings. Real estate expert Barbara Swartz of StagedHomes.com has built an international business around staging properties. Swartz's firm trains real estate agents and interior decorators in how to maximize the marketability and value of homes through more effective staging. A list of staging professionals who've earned accreditation from Staged Homes is available on www.StagedHomes.com.

Most staging principles apply across all price ranges; however, the upper-tier property often has special staging challenges. One of these staging challenges is a result of customization. Affluent homeowners can afford to add the special rooms, features, and other amenities which reflect the lifestyles they've chosen. They view their homes as absolutely perfect because they are perfect for them based on the lifestyle they lead. However, prospective buyers may look at these same fabulous features and view them as undesirable if they don't match their lifestyles. The homeowners may consider their exercise room, cigar room, and temperature controlled fur closet as adding tremendous value to their home. However if the buyer prospect would prefer to have a media room, home office, doesn't smoke, and objects to the wearing of fur, the seller's special features may actually get in the way of the sale.

If you need to broaden the appeal of a property by showing different uses for existing rooms, one approach is to find an interior designer with whom to work. Rather than redoing the rooms, ask the designer to create large picture boards illustrating the rooms used differently. It is not necessary that these design boards include paint chips or fabric swatches. All you need is an illustration of the envisioned room. For instance, the cigar room might be "redone" on the display board as a home office while the fur closet might be illustrated as a temperature controlled mini wine cellar. Mount these boards on large easels and place them at the entrance to the rooms or in the rooms. This allows prospects to see how a home might be adapted to different lifestyles.

Using decorator design boards is also an excellent way to stage rooms in a vacant house. Choose three or four key rooms and use the boards to add marketing pizzazz. This technique can also be used to avoid having to totally refurnish a large home. Some rooms are furnished; others are staged with design boards.

One strategy for covering the cost of the boards is to ask the seller to provide the buyer with a complimentary consultation with the decorator. The seller pays for this consultation. You can negotiate the cost of the boards as part of this consulting package. Since chances are good that the consultation will result in additional business for the decorator, you may be able to get the design boards and buyer's consultation at a very reasonable cost. In any case, the seller usually pays any staging costs.

Effective staging and the value of a home are closely linked. For example, a Los Angeles real estate agent was asked to sell a luxury home with a sound-proof shooting range in the basement. When pricing the home, he was not sure if he should add or subtract value for this unique feature. In fact, he was concerned that the shooting range might actually limit the marketability of the house. I agreed with him. After some discussion, we concluded that the shooting targets needed to be removed and any bullet holes in the walls filled. This would leave a big, empty sound-proof room. The resulting space could have been staged as a media room. This would have added value to the property, but an even easier solution was to market this space as a potential recording studio. An illustration of the room in use for a recording session was easily done. With Los Angeles as a music industry hot spot, this feature differentiated the house, added value for a specific target group, and the home was snapped-up by an affluent buyer who was looking for a property with a large recording studio.

Whether your listings need just a bit of accessorizing or a total redo, the time and money invested in staging can result in a faster sale at a higher price.

Keys to creating a successful property brochure

Your property brochure is a written sales presentation. Its effectiveness relies on good copy and photographs that showcase the home and the lifestyle it offers. Your positioning statement for the property will help you determine the brochure's theme, key points, and headlines. The brochure is also an opportunity to reinforce your positioning in the market, so you can include a small thumbnail photograph of yourself with your contact information. But, remember the brochure is first and foremost a selling tool for the home.

Expensive properties demand high-quality brochures. There are national vendors who specialize in full color real estate brochures and can refer a professional photographer to assist you. Compare quality, prices and turn-around time before selecting a vendor.

If you are not a good writer, find a freelance advertising writer or college advertising/marketing major and pay a small fee to have your copy edited. It will cost lots more if you ask them to create the copy from scratch. Draft it yourself, list all the amenities and features, and then let the expert rewrite it.

If you order color brochures, negotiate with the printer for color postcards to be printed at the same time. Once the brochure is on the press being printed, it is a simple matter to print other items as well. It requires a bit more press time and paper, but since the highest cost is preparing, inking, and then cleaning the press, it saves money to print everything you need at once. Design your postcards and other items when your brochure is designed. Even if the pieces are being produced digitally, there will usually be some savings by ordering multiple pieces at the same time.

Use professional photography and stage your homes for the photo shoot just as you do for an open house. Be on hand to direct the photographer. More people will see the photographs than will see the house, so the photographs will often determine whether someone is interested in the property or not. Bad photos and too few photos are perhaps the biggest marketing mistakes agents make. Quality photographs are absolutely key in effective property marketing. This is not the place to cut corners. Think of professional photographs as an investment in successful marketing, not an expense.

Plan the time of day for the photo session based on the specific property. Schedule the exterior photo shoot to coincide with the time of day that the front of the house is illuminated and not in the shadows. If you have a home with lots of shadows on the facade because of landscaping, you might ask the photographer to schedule the shoot for a cloudy day when shadows won't show (if timing allows) or when the light is soft (twilight). If you do a sunset or twilight shoot, turn on all the house lights for a warm and welcoming golden glow. Negotiate with your photographer so you have exclusive rights to the photographs.

Tips for writing better copy

Copy is another important element in the success of a brochure or ad. Unfortunately, copywriting is an area where most agents haven't had specific training and so they often opt to keep copy short, listing bullet points rather than writing descriptive copy. What a shame and what a disservice to the seller! Copy is your opportunity to tell the unique story of a home, to capture the attention of a targeted prospect, and create a desire to see the house. Bullet points won't accomplish this.

Stan Barron of Stan Barron Properties in Austin (TX) is a master copywriter – a Madison Avenue advertising guy who studied at the feet of the late David Ogilvy, a legendary ad man. Stan writes copy that works overtime in getting properties sold. You only have to look at some of the headlines, paragraphs, sentences, and phrases, he uses to have some sense of his approach to creating copy that gets attention, creates emotion, and causes buyers to act.

Think of the brochure or ad headline as your hook. You want it to catch the attention of the reader. In fact, five times more people will read your headline than will read the ad. That makes headlines pretty darn important. How could you resist wanting to know more about this house after seeing this headline of Stan's? "Ferrari-driving, high-tech recluse to sell Westlake hideaway: it's on two lots and has a 5-car garage"

Here's a description of a kitchen that almost makes you want to grab a sauce pan and start cooking: "This is one of those kitchens that is part of the entertaining space. It has cabinets that mimic furniture pieces and appliances that look like they belong in a restaurant. The stainless, duel-fuel, double oven, six-burner stove by Wolf is about the size of a Buick. The kitchen is a cornucopia of fun surfaces – stone floors laid in a French pattern, Desert Sage backsplash tiles with metal studs, and a second sink made of hammered copper in the massive wood-capped island. This section of the house will no doubt work like an invisible magnet when you have a party -- it will be the hub of all activity. And it is not hard to imagine being here early on weekend mornings with the aroma of bacon and eggs wafting in the air. One of the rituals you will fall into almost immediately is having breakfast with coffee and the newspaper by the pool, just like you do when you go on vacation." Stan's copy puts you in the home and lets you imagine what it would be like to live there. That's effective selling!

How about this paragraph about a home office? "While you

are still in the entry, look to your right, and you will notice an oversized set of glass-paneled doors. Through these doors lies an office that looks like it has been transported from a downtown law firm. There are wood floors, walls of built-in cabinets and tall ceilings lined with crown molding. You could stage the takeover of a Fortune 500 company from here."

Here's Stan's "close" for a builder's model home that is available fully furnished: "Here is a chance to get a "wow!" of a house. As a price comparison, imagine asking the builder to construct this same floor plan again for you. Tell the builder it must also be on a corner lot with a view. Ask the builder to match the same upgrades (like the $70,000 worth of wood floors, etc.) Finally, don't forget to mention that you require that the home be professionally landscaped, decorated and furnished. Just as you are finishing that last part, you might want to hold the phone away from your ear."

This opening paragraph has great appeal: "If you are a ready-to-act buyer, buckle-up because your anticipation is getting ready to surge into the 'red zone'. Welcome to 1234 Ridge Trail, Austin, Texas 78746. At last, here is a home that hits the jackpot on all key ingredients -- the location is close in, the architecture is dazzling, and the setting is shrouded in privacy."

Instead of simply saying "big lot," Stan writes, "This lot is 348' deep. Stop for just a second and put that into perspective – it is longer than a football field!" A private backyard with a pool? Stan says "Bathing suits are optional." "The home broadcasts few clues from the street," is a nice way of saying this one has no curb appeal. Stan quickly makes the point that a house has real architectural appeal, "If you were teaching an architecture class on how to blend design, textures and materials you could use this house when it is time to go on a field trip."

Here's some of what Stan says about his approach to real estate advertising and writing good copy. This is his "root canal rule" of advertising.

"Many of the most helpful tips for better advertising are so simple, they are overlooked. Here is one of the best. It has to do with putting things in their proper sequence. Pretend you are in the dentist's chair, and your root canal procedure is ready to get underway. The dentist shows you a tray with two items – a small spike and a shot of Novocain. Do you think it is important to know which of these comes first?

"There is a similar hierarchy in advertising, too. Laying out your sales pitch in the proper sequence can easily be the difference between success or failure. Before I write an ad for a house, I am always on the lookout for a single claim that is noteworthy -- one feature no competing house can match. One of Madison Avenue's most helpful insights is that five times as many people read headlines as they do the body copy. This means you put your most potent claim in the headline. (This is the equivalent of knowing that the Novocain comes first.) Reinforce that key claim again in the body copy, use a photo to illustrate it, and consider whether the floor plan, site plan, and location map might emphasize it as well. In other words, use as many reinforcing elements as possible to stress your key point. Simple? Very. Effective? Yes."

The same copy guidelines that work for brochure copy work for ad copy, too. Put them to work and all your sales communications will be more effective.

You may be thinking, "Do people really read long copy?" The answer is yes. The golden rule of advertising says, "Good long copy outsells good short copy every time."

Just be sure to keep your paragraphs short, use frequent subheads, make type large enough to be easily read, use adequate spacing between lines of copy, and make sure your copy is as compelling as Stan Barron's!

Author's Note: Institute members have the opportunity to do a hands-on advertising workshop with Stan Barron at special "Third Day" training sessions scheduled several times each year. See The Institute training schedule on our Website for details.

Using the Internet as a marketing tool

Consumers are finding their agents on the Web, researching properties online, and communicating with email. Research from NAR reveals that 24% of homebuyers say they first saw the home they purchased on the Internet. You must be Internet savvy, too. At the very least, here are a few of the things you'll need to do to utilize the Internet in your marketing.

Put your information on your firm's Website. You should have an agent profile on your firm's website. Think of this profile as a brochure promoting your services. Write benefit-oriented copy that is less about you and more about how you can help buyers and sellers achieve their real estate goals. If the format allows, use this opportunity to highlight your expertise in the upper-tier with a few testimonials.

Have your own Website and a plan to drive traffic to it. Content is king – it will help attract consumers, cause eyeballs to linger on your site, and should give prospects the information necessary to help them choose to work with you. If your market has implemented listing reciprocity and individual agent websites are allowed to feature all the MLS listing inventory, you may wish to add this feature to your site. The ability to display all the listings will help attract Web users and keep them on your site.

You may also want to:

- Consider a blog, but only if you are committed to managing it and posting frequently. It is worth taking the time to read and post comments to other real estate blogs.
- Participate in blogging and social networking sites such as ActiveRain.com

Put your listings Online with lots of information. Think of your website(s) as an opportunity to create detailed, electronic property brochures. Include a complete, well-written description of the property. Don't use real estate abbreviations; spell everything out. Feature multiple photographs of the property. Virtual tours may add value if they are well done, showcase the property effectively, and download quickly; however, research says that buyers would much rather see lots of photographs. Floor plans and site plans add value and should be included. Be sure to keep pricing and property status information current. Make it easy for prospects to contact you for additional information or for a showing appointment. Respond promptly. See www.StanBarronProperties for an example of an agent who does a great job of providing lots of information Online for each of his property listings.

Complete information about the property can also take the form of individual websites for each of your luxury listings. You might choose to use the property address (or name of property) as the domain name (e.g. www.196WhisperingWillowDrive. com). The individual website approach allows you to provide complete information on the property, plenty of visuals (photos, virtual tours, and videos), relevant links to schools and community information, transaction documents and more. For examples of property specific websites, go to www.Platinum-Homesites.com. Individual property sites are a smart approach to property marketing. Being able to offer a property-specific site to a seller is an effective listing tool.

In most markets, multiple listing systems offer listing reciprocity to broker members. This allows all the MLS listing inventory to be featured on participating brokers' websites. If your firm participates in reciprocity, you will want to be sure that each property description you submit to MLS is as effective with prospects as with agents. This also makes photographs of the property more important than ever. Consumers want complete information and multiple photographs of good quality. Ignore that fact and they'll skip right past your listing and look at others instead.

Consider posting your properties on luxury home websites such as www.LuxuryProperty.com. Sites like this attract lots of consumer eyeballs and can help you market not just locally, but globally.

Look for other opportunities to feature your listings online. Many real estate print publications will post your listing on their websites when you advertise in their publications. Be sure to ask your publication sales representative for exposure on the Web as well as in the printed publication. Many of these publication websites are aggregated by others. For instance, properties on the Unique Homes magazine site show up on more than two dozen other websites as well. This is valuable exposure. Look for other opportunities to syndicate and leverage your online listings.

E-mail new listing announcements to prospect groups. Keep your affluent center of influence updated on your new listings with short e-mail messages. Simple and concise emails typically work best. Be sure to provide easy to navigate links to complete property information on your website. Don't overdo. The level of your relationship with the recipient, the relevancy of the information, and the recipient's ability to opt-out are all important factors to consider. Make sure that you understand and comply with current commercial email and anti-spam regulations. Recognize too that time and attention are in short supply and that relevant, informative content is the key to maintaining your prospects' attention.

Establish Websites for the communities you farm. Creating a website for a neighborhood is both a community service and a powerful promotional tool for you. The site can include community photos, statistical information on real estate, a community events calendar, homeowner association information, school calendar, and, of course, information about your services and listings. Be sure to keep the website current.

To create your site, start by setting up the URL (or Web address). Do a search for the neighborhood name you wish to use. You can register the name Online for a reasonable fee. Ask your website developer to design a simple, inexpensive site for you. Post community information, link to schools and other resources. Coordinate with the local homeowners association by offering to post their newsletter, community event announcements, and other information on the site. The more of a resource the site is for the community, the better marketing tool it will be for you. Promote the neighborhood website in your farming materials, in relevant advertising, and in property brochures.

Your neighborhood site is a great place to post your regular market updates containing information on the neighborhood housing market. This helps reinforce your reputation as the neighborhood expert. If you're an Institute member, this is another way to use the charts created on the FREE My Market Graphs™ software on the Institute's website. Post any market updates you create on your personal website too.

Use on-the-go technology to access MLS. Technology can help you provide better service. Many technological devices provide Internet access, allowing you to have the MLS at your fingertips. This provides listing information on the go. If you are out with a buyer who has a question about a home you happen to drive by, you can check MLS to see price and current status. You can pull up the contact information and call for an appointment if the buyer wishes. You will also have the ability to pull up information on other relevant properties. Having the MLS data at your fingertips can save time and help you deliver the level of service your affluent clients and customers expect.

Network Online. The Web is brimming with special interest websites and blogs. Some of these sites offer the opportunity to network directly with potential prospects or to advertise your listings inexpensively. For instance, if you specialize in equestrian properties, do an Online search for sites that relate to horse ownership. Check out the sites for opportunities to post a notice or add a classified ad about your listings.

Posting thoughtful comments that demonstrate expertise and professionalism on relevant blogs and other sites can be a good way to build your reputation Online and drive quality traffic to your site.

The Internet is a fabulous resource, use it!

Broker Opens are important

Be sure to schedule an open house for brokers and take the time to personally invite the agents in your community who specialize in the luxury home market. This "broker open" can also be a good way to gather feedback about the property. Create a small card that you can give to real estate agents as they arrive to see the home. Jokingly tell them it is their ticket to leave the house. Keep questions short and simple so that it can be filled in quickly. Have some extra pencils handy. You may get more honest feedback if you make responses anonymous by providing a basket to hold completed cards.

1234 Luxury Lane

Your expertise and opinion are valuable to me.
Please take a minute to give me your honest feedback with regard to this new listing:

Pricing	__Excellent __Good __Fair __Poor
How well it shows	__Excellent __Good __Fair __Poor
Probability you would show	__Excellent __Good __Fair __Poor

Comments _____

_____

Use VIP, invitation-only special events

At the entry level of the upper-tier or with new home properties, it may be desirable to hold traditional open houses. In the higher price ranges, security issues and the brevity of the qualified prospect list will make invitation-only VIP events (usually called real estate soirees) more appropriate. If a special event to showcase the home and the lifestyle it represents is part of your marketing plan, you will want to talk to your sellers about adding their friends, acquaintances, and business associates who may lead a similar lifestyle to the list of invitees. In addition, you will want to consider if there are special target groups based on the location or amenities the home offers. Think of this event as a party to sell the house.

Here's how a soiree might work: Mojitos in hand, the guests nibble skewers of spicy shrimp as they discuss what's happening with real estate prices and eye the home that is the setting for the posh event.

The hand-picked guests are invited to stroll though the property, admire the ocean view, tour the 2000 bottle wine cellar, test the theatre seats in the media room, and admire the exotic wood paneling in both his and her home offices. However, this is not your typical cocktail party. It is a real estate soiree, or what is often called "the party to sell the house," and the listing agent is hoping at least one guest will leave with the intent to make an offer.

Increasingly in today's challenging market the agents marketing luxury homes are looking for ways to draw attention to their properties and are recognizing the value of invitation-only special events which highlight a home's lifestyle, attract affluent prospects (and their agents), and create buzz in the marketplace. Upper-tier buyers are looking for properties which offer just the right lifestyle and real estate soirees are all about showcasing lifestyles.

Institute member, Vivian Bridaham, with Sotheby's International Realty in Jackson (WY) sells multimillion dollar ranch and resort properties by using fine art shows to draw prospects to her special VIP open house events. Honore Frumentino with Koenig and Strey GMAC in suburban Chicago doesn't just show her multi-million dollar listings, she uses exclusive VIP marketing events to create buzz in the market and often gets local media coverage for her properties as a result. Danny Veal with Stirling Sotheby's International Realty in Winter Park (FL) recently hosted a soiree and partnered with other purveyors of luxury products to create a home marketing event worth tens of thousands of dollars, but it cost him virtually nothing. These three Certified Luxury Home Marketing Specialists are among the successful upper-tier agents using the real estate soiree as an important marketing tool.

Here are a few things to consider to make your real estate soirees more successful.

Target the invitees. You'll probably want to invite your area's top luxury home agents and their prospects, as well as qualified prospects from your own center of influence. Since the friends and associates of the homeowner may lead a similar lifestyle, be sure to take the time to sit down with your sellers and compile their list of suggested invitees. You may also want to add to your guest list by including specific categories of people for whom the house might have special interest. For example, identify and include top architects for a home with architectural significance. A home near a private airport might have special appeal to owners of personal jets. Wine collectors may have special interest in a home with a large wine cellar.

Leverage the event by teaming up with other purveyors of luxury goods or services. Inviting others who sell luxury products and services to participate in these events can add marketing value, help draw the right crowd, and often offset the costs. If you have a home with a wonderful wine cellar, why not ask a local dealer in fine wines to co-host the event. He or she could stage a wine tasting, add excitement with a drawing for a bottle of bubbly, and provide an invitation list of wealthy wine connoisseurs to be invited to the event. You might also consider asking the wine merchant to suggest a list of wines. Then, price the home with and without a cellar full of fine wines. This marketing twist might even generate some press coverage for your listing.

Join forces with a non-profit. If you or your sellers have a favorite charity, you might wish to turn your soiree into a fund raising event for charity. This allows you to give back to the community while marketing your listing. The charity may help you plan and promote the event and will add their major donors and other prospects to your invitation list. A charitable event may also attract the media and generate some press coverage for your house party. Stage an auction for the charity. List a home with its own putting green and stage an afternoon CEO putting tournament for charity. The big benefit – the CEOs are exposed to your listing.

Co-hosting with a carefully selected non-profit group generates free publicity and can increase attendance and exposure for the home. The non-profit group also brings important resources, including people who can serve as room monitors while the house is open. Be sure sellers know to put away small valuables and breakables during the event. A local museum, historic preservation society, opera, or symphony group would be an example of a non-profit organization that might plan a members-only event with you.

Think like Martha Stewart. The real estate soiree isn't just an open house, think of it as an event to celebrate the lifestyle the home offers. Create a theme that ties to the home, and then build your event around that theme. If the house has a wonderful home theatre, you might plan an Oscars party. Have a classic award winning movie playing. Book a pianist to play Oscar award winning movie themes. Serve James Bond martinis, Casablanca cocktails, Scarlett O'Hara sweet potato flan – you get the idea. Whatever your theme, use it for your party invitations and decorations as well.

The home and its amenities should prompt lots of ideas for a special event. Market a home with a fabulous catering kitchen or fully-equipped outdoor kitchen by hosting a gourmet cooking demonstration by a well-known local chef. The goal is to create a memorable event, showcase the property, generate buzz, and give prospects a taste of what it would be like to own the home.

Set the stage for a sale. When you go to the trouble of planning a real estate soiree, or extreme open house as they are sometimes called, you want to be sure the home shows perfectly, so be sure it is well staged. Security should also be a consideration. Small valuables should be locked away. Room monitors are also a good idea. Utilize your team members or recruit newer agents from your office to assist. Be sure everyone can talk intelligently about the home and its features. Pay attention to the details: Must invitees RSVP? Will you need a valet parking service? Do you need to rent glasses and other party ware? Do you expect the owners' staff to assist at the event? Did you remember to invite the media? Plan well and your event will not only be a social success, it will be a marketing success as well. The party to sell the house should do just that, help SELL the house.

Adapt your event to the specific property. Maureen Kennedy, a member of The Institute for Luxury Home Marketing in Piedmont (CA) took the soiree idea and tweaked it for a home that needed updating. Her upscale listing needed serious updating, so instead of a party, she hosted a "Renovator's Open House" with professional design experts on hand to discuss remodeling options.

The idea came about when Maureen put herself in the position of a buyer prospect for this particular home and realized that the challenge in getting this house sold was going to be helping people understand that a whole-house renovation could be manageable, both financially and emotionally. Once she figured that out, a "Renovator's Open House" occurred to her as the solution.

Maureen included four experts in the open event -- an architect, a builder in the midst of his second whole-house renovation in the same area, a color consultant, and a painting company.

Four hundred people come through the house over two weekends of Saturday and Sunday open houses. Maureen said some were looky-loos, but many were potential buyers who had already self-selected for a renovation opportunity. Organizing the event, including name tags, took about an hour more than a typical open house. She also spent another hour organizing "goody bags" for the four vendors as a thank-you gift.

Maureen's strategy paid off when multiple bids came in for her $1.5 million listing and it sold in less than two weeks for 18% above the asking price.

Other marketing ideas

Keep your eyes and ears open for other ways to promote your listings. For instance, if you have a unique property which was designed by a well-known architect, has celebrity owners, or is priced in the multi-million-dollar price range, you might consider contacting *The Wall Street Journal* and *Architectural Digest*. The Journal has a "Property of the Week" feature which runs in both the printed and Online versions of the paper. The magazine has a monthly residential real estate section featuring very special homes for sale. Both of these features are content as opposed to advertising.

Architectural Digest is a beautiful vehicle for promoting truly exceptional properties with international appeal. *Architectural Digest's* homes for sale section is called "Estates for Sale: Editors Select Properties Around the World" and features exotic properties as diverse as a villa in a Venetian lagoon, a home on the French Riviera designed by the architect of the Eiffel tower, and the penthouse of a Manhattan Beaux Arts Bank building constructed in 1907 and converted to private residences. If you have a truly world-class property, this special magazine section is an option to explore for very high end properties.

These publications offer the benefit of readers with the right demographics – they can afford to buy luxury homes. Remember, both these publications are looking for truly exceptional homes, celebrity-owned properties, or homes with newsworthy stories.

Properties with interesting stories or other news value lend themselves to being marketed through public relations. Don't forget local, regional and national media when you are planning marketing strategies for your special listings.

Chapter Fourteen
Delivering Quality Service

Quality in a product or service is not what the supplier puts in. It is what the customer gets out and is willing to pay for...customers pay only for what is of use to them and gives them value. Nothing else constitutes quality. – Peter Drucker

Remember that the buying and selling process really doesn't differ much by price range; however, the luxury market is more demanding of your professionalism, communication skills, and ability to get the job done. You are dealing with successful individuals who have high expectations for themselves and who will hold you to the highest service standards. Remember that today's affluent consumers have service expectations created by other industries that set service benchmarks. Your service will be measured against those benchmarks. In short, when you work with rich buyers and rich sellers, you'd better be good!

In Chapter 9, we looked at the importance of positioning yourself as unique and better able to meet the needs of rich buyers and sellers. Creating this perception in the minds of your clients and customers and then delivering on that promise will mean that buyers and sellers will want to work with you, will be willing to pay a full or premium price, and will be eager to refer you. Quality service is an important part of living up to the promise of being unique and better.

Before we talk about the specifics of creating value for the consumer, it is important to understand the three stages of success and how they relate to value creation.

Understand the three stages of success

In real estate, success comes from understanding and meeting the needs of your clients and customers. As you develop your ability to do that, you will pass through three levels of success.

The agent in the first stage of success is average. He or she has basic skills and generally doesn't focus on specific market segments or work to build special competencies. Because the average agent doesn't define and target market opportunities, he or she must be all things to all people and handle whatever business presents itself. After a while, the average agent's market tends to define itself. For example, if you sell a first time homebuyer and do a good job, chances are that client will refer a friend. The next thing you know, you are working with lots of first-timers and working in neighborhoods of entry-level homes. This might be terrific, unless you would prefer to be working in higher price ranges and specializing in golf course properties.

Success Stage 1.
THE AVERAGE AGENT
↑
Acceptable Service
↑
"All Things to All People"
↑
Basic Competence

The next level of success is illustrated by the Top Producer who has targeted special market segments and has developed market and customer knowledge specific to those niches. At this level, the agent better understands how to meet customer expectations and provides really good service.

Success Stage 2.
THE TOP PRODUCER
↑
Meeting Customer Needs
↑
Really Good Service
↑
Developing Target Markets
↑
Special Expertise
↑
Strong Competence

Agents at the third stage rate "best in the business" recognition. They not only have targeted special niches, but have developed so much expertise and market knowledge that they are unique. As a result of these unique abilities, they are able to offer additional value and special services that exceed client expectations. Success stage three is the level you want to attain.

Success Stage 3.
THE BEST IN THE BUSINESS
↑
Surprise and WOW Customers
↑
Outstanding Service
↑
Ability to Create Value
↑
Defined Target Markets
↑
Unique Abilities

Focus on creating value for the consumer

Clarify expectations. The time to establish expectations is during your initial interaction with a buyer and during your listing presentation to a seller. An excellent way to do this is with a service guarantee checklist that outlines what you'll do step-by-step for the buyer or seller. This checklist can be even stronger if it outlines the steps and attaches a benefit statement to each point. Keep your guarantee realistic. Don't raise expectations you can't meet. Instead, under-promise and over-deliver.

Here's my guarantee to you:

- I'll prepare a competitive market analysis with information on current homes for sale and relevant sold properties. This information, plus advice on pricing to maximize buyer interest and bottom line returns for you, means you'll have the information you need to make the best decision on pricing your home.

- Together we'll tour your home and discuss how to "stage" it so that it can be shown most effectively

- Your property will be entered into the Multiple Listing System, which means information about your home is available to virtually all the agents in the market. This maximizes the exposure for your property.

- Etc.

As you walk them through your service guarantee, you'll also be discovering how their expectations match up with the list. In doing this, you'll discover issues before they can become problems. For instance, if you have an assistant who often handles calls and specific tasks for buyers and sellers, your clients may have questions about why they can't always deal directly with you. It's important to answer questions like those at the beginning.

You'll also want to be sure your expectations are communicated. If you expect sellers to leave the house during showings, you'll need to express that and perhaps explain why. If the best way to communicate with you is on your cell phone or via e-mail, now's the time to let them know that. Sharing expectations also opens the communication process.

Instill confidence. Recognize that good communication and personal integrity will help ensure that the consumer feels good about working with you. Here are five things that will go a long way toward helping you establish credibility and create confidence in the consumer's mind.

- Show up on time
- Listen
- Do what you promise
- Admit mistakes and fix them quickly
- Remember that manners matter

Care about your client and work to connect. Be personable. We all want to work with someone we like. To some extent we are all selling a relationship; because, in an initial interaction, it is easier to evaluate a relationship than it is to measure competency. Ask yourself if you would want to work with you.

Create a positive experience. How can you enhance the experience for the customer? What can you do to lessen the stress, make the process more interesting, or add an element of positive surprise? It's also important to look for vendors who are focused on ways to add value. For instance, Houston-based Stewart Title Company has a special division for closing fine homes and estates and offers an environment and service level to please the most demanding client. One of their services is providing translators for buyers and sellers for whom English is not the primary language; documents can also be translated. This is an excellent value-add for your international clientele. In short, effectively working with upper-tier clients requires creative thinking and more individualized attention, special services and marketing than traditional real estate practices.

Nash & Company specializes in the resorts in the Vail Valley of Colorado and Naples (FL), Broker/owner Jo Ellen Nash says, "Our philosophy is to offer clients concierge level service. We have shifted our focus and allocated more of our marketing budget to client perks and benefits versus newspaper or magazine advertising, which we have found to be far less effective."

Jo Ellen and her team take the time to really know their clients' hobbies, interests and families. This goes a long way toward establishing and maintaining long-term relationships and loyalty. Keeping detailed records and client database enables them to stay in touch in ways that are meaningful. For example, if they know a client enjoys wine, they may arrange to have a wine and cheese basket waiting for them when they arrive in town, send them a letter with an article about a new great wine Website, or provide a complimentary subscription to The Wine Enthusiast. If the client loves fly-fishing, they'll arrange for access to a private section of the Eagle River, which offers blue-ribbon fishing, perhaps even hire a guide. "We have found that this type of personalized attention is more effective than general past client 'keep in touch' letters that are the same for every client," explains Jo Ellen.

Acting as a concierge for clients also involves referring them to various businesses and services as needs arise. "They trust us to connect them with the best sources – they don't always live in Vail full time and don't have the local knowledge that we do," Jo Ellen explains. "We may help them find babysitters, moving companies (we have our own complimentary moving van) interior designers, handyman and construction contractors, architects, physicians or whomever else they need. We also provide them with complimentary use of our Internet, fax and copier services at our office if they need a business environment while at their vacation home."

There is also a Nash and Company limousine which is available to take clients to and from the airport. Although Jo Ellen says she doesn't often use it to show homes, her clients love being able to reserve it for special events like birthdays and anniversaries. And of course it also serves as a moving billboard for the company -- a very posh one!

Jo Ellen has also developed a market update newsletter (View From the Top), a regular source of communication with high-end clients which provides them with inside information and statistics on the upper-tier market. It also establishes the team's credibility and provides important exposure for their upper-tier property listings.

This level of service is what affluent buyers and sellers expect. Jo Ellen says, "Thinking and serving your clients creatively and meaningfully will pay off huge dividends. It has for us!"

Say thank you. Manners matter. When you are trusted by a client to help with his or her home sale or purchase, a verbal thank you is required. A hand-written note and thank-you gift are always appropriate as well. An annual thank-you event for your customers serves the dual purpose of showing your appreciation for their business and helping you maintain contact.

Ask how you did. You may think you did a good job, but what does your client think? You won't know for certain unless you ask. A short written survey allows him or her to give you feedback in a way that promotes honest comments. Be sure to also ask for the nicest thing he or she can honestly say about your service and permission to use his or her quotes in your marketing. Then add the positive comments to your testimonial book, Website testimonials section, presentation materials, or other marketing pieces.

Stay in touch, stay in touch, stay in touch. Make it a point to contact your past clients and customers on a regular basis. Let them know you are available to help with their real estate needs and ask for referrals. The goal is to build an ongoing relationship.

Chapter Fifteen

Meeting Special Challenges

Targeting the upper-tier in a small community

Smaller markets may not have many luxury properties. In this case, your goal is to capture as many of them as possible – to become the dominant agent in the upper price range.

Tie the luxury home target market to other market niches that might logically mesh with it. For instance, if high-priced properties are clustered in a particular neighborhood that also has homes in other price ranges, work the neighborhood. Maybe your luxury buyers and sellers are primarily corporate executives. If so, target the corporate and relocation markets. Find a geographic farm area priced just below the upper-tier and hope to capture buyers moving out and moving up. If your top properties are waterfront or golf course homes, focus on those special markets even though not all the properties will be upper-tier. In summary, combine related niches with the upper-tier niche and you'll have a solid strategy.

Unless your market has a very large luxury segment, you may find that you need to work other price ranges, too. If you are concerned about being a luxury specialist and serving a wide spectrum of price ranges, don't be. It's easy to explain that while you specialize in the upper-tier market, you work other price ranges by referral and for repeat and other special clients. And, of course, you provide your very best service to everyone.

Marketing historic real estate

Many markets have historic properties that may command high prices. The National Trust for Historic Preservation offers real estate professionals a variety of resources. A special program, open to real estate agents regardless of company affiliation, includes training covering architectural styles from early colonial through art deco. It provides education on historic preservation legislation and ordinances, tax incentives, and the requirements for inclusion in the National Register of Historic Places. If you work in a market with numerous historic properties, this training will strengthen your expertise in the historic home niche. Course participants are also given a six-month membership in the National Trust, a certificate of completion, and approved verbiage to use in personal promotion. Agents who attend the program are listed with their contract information on the National Trust's Website, www.nationaltrust.org. That's also where you'll find a link to the training schedule, and registration information.

The National Trust for Historic Preservation also publishes Preservation magazine which is an excellent medium for advertising your historic properties. It's affordable and properties also appear on the Trust's Website. Visit www.nationaltrust.org for information. This is also a great resource if you have a buyer who is looking for an historic property.

The National Register of Historic Places was authorized under the National Historic Preservation Act of 1966 and is administered by the Department of the Interior's National Park Service. It is the nation's official list of historically significant structures.

A National Register designation mandates that a property must be considered in the planning of federal or federally assisted projects impacting the registered property and qualifies that site for financial assistance from the government when preservation funds are available. Properties may qualify for special mortgages, grants, and tax credits. Remember that there are restrictions on physical changes to these properties.

To learn more about the National Register, visit its Website, www.cr.nps.gov/nr. It includes information on the more than 70,000 listed properties and information on how to nominate a property.

Working with other experts as part of your client's team

When dealing with affluent individuals, you will often be just one of the experts they employ to assist them in their real estate decision-making. They may want to turn to their CPA and estate planner to discuss the tax consequences of a home purchase, or for advice about how to hold ownership based on estate and inheritance issues. An attorney, tax accountant, business manager, private banker, estate trustee, or financial consultant may also be part of the decision process. Working though the maze of players and their responsibilities can make the buy/sell decision process more complex and require your patience.

If you're lucky, the client will manage this process. If he or she looks to you to do that, then you'll have to keep things moving forward diplomatically. Recognize the role that everyone plays in the process and avoid stepping on toes while you work to facilitate the process for the client. Keep communication open and flowing among participants. Help keep everyone focused on the client's goal. Be sure you understand the contribution the client expects each participant to make and be sure the client understands the time frame in which things must be finalized to keep a scheduled closing (or negotiation) on track.

Success in the luxury home market is about positioning yourself as THE expert and then delivering on that promise—which means knowing the luxury market better than the competition and getting results for buyers and sellers. Once you've done that, your reputation will create opportunities and referrals. In the meantime, work on building your competencies, look for the unique skills and tools that may give you an edge and use them.

Selling luxury homes at auction

Auctions are no longer just associated with distress sales or bargain basement prices. A well-planned real estate auction can generate premium prices for homes. Sellers of unique or extremely expensive properties that are difficult to appraise and have high monthly costs may want to consider working with you and an auction company in hopes of a speedy sale and maximum price. A quick auction sale can reduce marketing time and consequently cut an owner's carrying costs such as mortgage expense, maintenance and insurance expenses, and taxes. Properties in high- inventory markets may also benefit by using an auction to capture attention. Tony A. Isbell, president of RealtyBid.com sold more than 12,000 commercial, investment, and luxury residential properties over more than 20 years as the practice of auctioning luxury residences has grown.

According to Isbell, there are there are three common types of auctions. Generally, auctions are assumed to be reserve auctions unless explicitly advertised otherwise. In a reserve auction, there is no minimum bid. The seller is not obligated to sell the property but has the right to accept or reject the highest bid.

In an absolute auction, a sale is guaranteed. The property will go to the highest bidder, regardless of the price. The absolute auction usually attracts the most bidders because prospective buyers are hoping for a bargain. With lots of bidders, a competitive bidding environment is often created, which results in a top price. A minimum bid auction is just that – only bids above a minimum advertised amount are accepted.

Auction houses will work with a listing agent to plan and conduct a successful luxury home auction. This technique is growing in popularity.

Isbell describes the typical auction event as starting six to eight weeks in advance with advertising, usually paid for by the seller. Free press coverage is generally sought for the auction as well. A property brochure is created and mailed to a target prospect list developed by the real estate agent and the auction company. The property is available for scheduled showing appointments and should also be available for viewing on the Internet with virtual tours and multiple photographs.

The day of the auction, the home is open, and bids are accepted from registered bidders who typically must post a five percent deposit in certified funds. When the winning bid is established, the bidder must sign a purchase contract and set a closing date, typically within six weeks. All other deposit checks are returned to other bidders.

Not only are auctions growing in numbers, they are moving Online. General consumer auction sites such as eBay have grown in popularity and made people more comfortable with the Online auction process. RealtyBid.com capitalizes on this Online auction success by offering Internet auctions for luxury home properties on its Website, www.RealtyBid.com

Michael Keracher, RealtyBid.com's executive vice president of sales and marketing, says, "In the past when I would visit owners of luxury properties, they had several concerns about traditional auctions including privacy issues, the intrusiveness and hype of an auction, plus costs and risks. Internet platforms (like RealtyBid.com's) allow an auction to happen in cyberspace, not at the property. This is less intrusive and is a huge privacy benefit to sellers. It is also about half the price of a traditional auction. An Online auction takes place over 30 days instead of just a few minutes. If the property does not meet its minimum price, the auction can simply be extended."

The Internet auction is an interesting marketing tool that may be a match for selective luxury properties and sellers. For more detailed information on how luxury home auctions work and what the real estate agent's role is in the auction process, check out the following NAR information sites:

Auction Information Center:
http://www.realtor.org/auction/index.html

Auction Field Guide:
http://www.realtor.org/libweb.nsf/pages/fg418

Selling the very expensive property

As of mid-year 2007, there were six properties on the market in the US priced at $100 million or more. One of those properties – "Tranquility" – on the Nevada side of Lake Tahoe was listed with Institute member Shari Chase of Chase International. Shari has lots of experience marketing very expensive listings. She has set the record for the most expensive property sold in the U.S. several times. Here are just a few of Shari's insights about the unique challenges of marketing very expensive homes.

"The number one consideration when handling these types of properties is to be discreet. The buyers, sellers, and everyone in your network appreciates it. Great resources and high standards are critical as well. Even your marketing plan should be discreet. We decided to limit the information we would share with the general public based on the fact that the person buying this home probably would not want all the details known. We decided to have three levels of information to provide for the three levels of inquiring prospects – the general public, serious inquiries, and qualified buyers. We then segmented the photographs, print materials, and Web site, according to the level of interest and qualification.

"The first level of information which is for the general public has an abstract style and limited details. We reveal very little about the home at this level, sticking to just basic information and teasers about what is included with the purchase.

"The second level is for more serious inquiries or top producing agents that may know a potential client. For this level, we produced a 16-page booklet and included more pictures and details. The home is truly a work of art, so to convey the artistic feel of the home, we decided not to write descriptions for the booklet; instead, we used Japanese-style Haiku poetry to accompany the photos. This booklet went to people we felt would know potential buyers for property at this price point – top-producing agents, attorneys, accountants, wealth managers, etc.

"The third level marketing piece is much more detailed and is strictly reserved for the potential buyer who fully qualifies.

"We also created multiple Web sites that are available depending on level of interest and buyer's qualifications.
"We work with an outsourced PR agency that works with us

exclusively. They have come to know us, our style, our demographics, and where we are pulling people from. We brainstormed with the PR agency on when and how to introduce the property and strategically place information across the globe. As far as purchasing advertising, we haven't had to. We had a complete PR plan designed before we brought the home to the market. We were positioned to be featured in the Wall Street Journal first and then the Associated Press picked it up. Since then, the home has been featured by RCN networks (the BBC of Latin American radio), numerous national and international magazines, CNBC High Net Worth, AOL, Forbes.com and more. We've generated so much free publicity that we've had to turn away camera crews. They all wanted to come in and film. While it may have been good for their shows, the real issue is that everything needs to benefit the home. If a camera crew is walking around filming just anything, we lose control of what is being presented.

"We prefer to maintain full control of everything. Many years ago, I shared the expense of advertising with the seller but never really felt this was a good idea. I like to control the marketing and advertising myself without being financially obligated to the seller, or obligated to try suggestions from the seller that I don't believe in. That said, I do encourage input from the sellers and sometimes an idea I have not thought of surfaces.

"Networking with other top luxury home professionals is important. Fortunately, we are lucky to have the talent in the luxury market that we have today. The other agents and brokers that we work with are phenomenal."

Shari's comment about networking with other luxury agents reinforces just how important networking can be as part of an overall marketing plan.

Chapter Sixteen
The Second-Home & Resort Markets

Second-home market offers opportunities

Just as the luxury market has been a growing part of the national home sale market, so has the second-home market been on the upswing. These markets overlap, as the buyers of vacation and investment homes are generally affluent – median income of the typical vacation home buyer in 2006 was $102,200. Depending upon your location, vacation and investment properties can be a large part of your local market and represent excellent opportunities to work with affluent buyers and sellers, over and above helping them buy and sell primary residences.

The vacation market offers two additional opportunities. There is the chance to work in multiple vacation/resort markets (sometimes requiring licensing in multiple jurisdictions). You can also refer your affluent buyers to vacation/resort locales, delivering service to your buyers and generating referral fees for yourself. There can also be an international aspect to this market with foreign buyers coming to the U.S. and U.S. buyers looking for properties abroad.

Two different segments – investment and vacation

The second home market grew slowly in the last half of the

1990's, but, in the years between 2001 and 2004, second home sales more than doubled, jumping from about 450,000 units annually to 881,000 units. These sales figures include both the investment and vacation property market segments. Much of this overall "second home" growth was actually in investment properties, as investors and speculators shifted dollars into real estate and out of stocks, bonds and other asset categories in the years after the dot com crash.

By 2004 and 2005, the investor market had become rife with speculation. In many markets, contracts were being flipped before closing, appreciation was at double digit levels, and get-rich-quick training programs were marketed to people ready to leverage every dollar they could scrape up to invest in residential real estate – whether it met traditional investment guidelines or not. Many investment properties were not being purchased to be held as investments, they were being purchased to sell ASAP. The desire for a quick buck was a prime factor driving the investor market, creating market conditions that were not sustainable in the long term. In 2005, 27.7 % of all home sales in the U.S. were investments. Another 12.2% were vacation homes. The two categories together represented about 40% of all homes sold that year. By 2006, the investment category was softening. As a category, it slipped to 22% of homes sold that year.

Second Home Sales as a Percent of Total Home Sales

2005 Second Home Sales	2006 Second Home Sales
27.7 % Investment homes	22 % Investment home
12.2 % Vacation homes	14 % Vacation homes
39.9 % of Total home sales	36 % of Total home sales

NAR Investment and Homebuyers Survey, released 2007

The vacation/resort market is a different story. There is certainly an overlap between the two categories, but as the reasons for purchase of investment and vacation homes are mostly different, it makes sense to look at them separately. From 2005 to 2006, vacation/resort sales increased from 12.2 % to 14% of all sales, an increase of 4.7%. As boomers have moved into prime income years and are looking ahead to retirement, vacation home sales have surged. Inheritance, home appreciation, rising wealth, creative loans, and exciting vacation and resort property options have all played a role in the growth of vacation home sales. The points below (from NAR's research) reveal a bit more about who is buying in this important market niche and what they are purchasing.

Fast Facts about vacation home buyers

- The "typical" vacation home buyer is a young boomer, age 44
- Median income is $102,200
- Median home price is $200,000 (down a bit from 2005)
- Twenty five percent of vacation home buyers pay all cash
- About a third (32%) buy 500 miles or more away from their primary residence
- Another 42% buy less than 100 miles away from primary home
- Single family homes are purchased by 67%, 21% buy condos
- Twelve percent of vacation home buyers report owning two vacation homes, 2% say they own three or more
- What type location do they prefer? (Multiple answers were accepted.)
    - 66% Close proximity to an ocean, river, or lake
    - 39% Recreation or sports activities nearby
    - 38% Close to vacation or resort area
    - 31% Near mountains or other natural attractions

- Urban or Country properties?
  - 29% Bought rural properties
  - 24% Bought in resort communities
  - 22% Bought suburban residences
  - 10% Bought urban or Center City properties

NAR resources

Recognizing the importance of this market segment, NAR offers a long list of resources to agents who want to work with resort and second home buyers and sellers. NAR's resort home page, www.REALTOR.org/Resort, provides industry-related links and up-to-date news.

In addition, The Resort & Second-Home Real Estate Forum is an educational forum to help you discover emerging issues in the resort and second-home market as well as learn about new business practices in marketing and branding. Realtors® specializing in the resort and second-home market also have the opportunity to earn the Resort & Second-Home Property Specialist (RSPS) certification. For information about the designation training and to register, go to www.coursecalendar.com. An annual Resort Symposium is another benefit of getting involved in NAR's Resort and Second Home program.

Chapter Seventeen

Getting Started in the Luxury Home Niche

New to luxury home marketing?
Share a listing with an experienced agent

You've decided to target the upper-tier and you've found a good listing prospect, but you're concerned that your inexperience and lack of a track record in the higher price ranges may hinder your ability to capture the listing. Why not find an experienced upper-tier agent with your company and offer to partner on your first transaction? You provide the prospect and do the work; he or she provides credibility and serves as your mentor for this transaction.

Naturally, you split the fee. To avoid misunderstandings, agree upon the responsibilities and the fee-sharing upfront.

You and the experienced agent should carefully plan the marketing consultation presentation and work together on the market analysis and the marketing plan. As an agent starting in the luxury market, you will probably want to perform these planning tasks yourself under the guidance of the experienced pro. This will help you maximize your own learning.

Since the prospect is yours, you'll want to take the initial lead in the listing presentation and then hand off to the more experienced agent. You should:

- Thank the sellers for the opportunity to meet with them about marketing their home,
- Introduce the experienced agent and highlight the agent's credibility and track record of success in the upper-tier arena.
- Discuss why and how you will work together as a team to market the property. Stress the benefits of having both of you working for them.
- Use "we" terminology to reinforce the fact that you'll be working together as a marketing team.

The presentation of the market analysis or CMA and the discussion/negotiation of marketing price with the seller will probably best be done by the experienced agent

In presenting the written marketing plan, you may to wish to highlight who will be responsible for implementing each marketing task. You will probably assume most of the responsibility for implementation.

Highlight the experienced agent's ability to network with other agents who specialize in the higher price range (locally and internationally), and let your partner explain why that is so important. Emphasize his or her contacts in the community and how that center of influence will be utilized in your marketing plan.

It is not necessary that the presentation be evenly divided, but each team member should have the opportunity to establish credibility and rapport. Clearly position the two of you as a team providing added value to the client. Be sure your client knows who will be the primary contact.

Remember that first impressions are very important. You must look professional and project confidence and professionalism. Don't wing it; be prepared. Then, to differentiate your, your listing presentation must sell these things:

- Your joint competencies. Why are you the best agents for the job? Your teammate's experience, training, market knowledge, pricing ability and contacts can help accomplish the seller's objectives Add your enthusiasm, hard work, and creativity, and you have a super sales duo. (This is about why you can accomplish their real estate goals more than it is about you —be confident, but leave your ego at home)

- Your company. Talk about the company, its resources, advertising, relocation connections, or other important features, and how these things work to help you assist them in marketing their home.

- A written marketing plan customized for the property. Luxury home sellers want to know exactly how you plan to market their home. Saying, "I'll promote your home," isn't enough. They want to know how, where, and when.

You'll probably want to let the experienced agent ask for the listing. You can hand the client the pen!

Here's a sample script explaining the joint approach (just to get you started).

"My goal is to do the best possible job for you. To maximize my marketing power, I've asked Sally Salespro, who is one of the top luxury home experts in our community, to act as a special consultant in the marketing of your home. Sally and I will work as a team. Her extensive experience, expertise, and market contacts combined with my aggressive marketing will be a powerful combination. Together we can implement a marketing plan designed to market your luxury property effectively.

"An aggressive newer agent with the time and energy to really focus on getting the job done for you...PLUS an experienced agent with incredible market savvy and contacts in the luxury home market... PLUS a special marketing plan for your home...that's a combination that will get you the results you want."

Agent's Getting Started Work Sheet

What's Your Action Plan?

What will you do to jump-start your business in the upper-tier...or to take it to the next level? Here are some ideas to spark your own planning process.

Step I. Analyze the upper-tier market: Gather the key statistics
(If there are other agents in your office who are also targeting the upper-tier, team up for the information-gathering step...divide the tasks and share the results.)

- Define your market area

- Identify top 10% of sales/listings in last 12 months

- Break this top 10% into logical price bands

- Calculate for each price band
  Number of sales (buyers)
  Sale to expiration ratio
  Average days on market
  List to sales price differential
  Percent new versus resale (an estimate)
  Average term of listing the competition is negotiation (this may be a "best guess" estimate)

- Make charts to illustrate these statistics

- As an Institute member, remember you can do this Online with the My Market Graphs software found on our Institute website: www.LuxuryHomeMarketing.com. You collect the data from MLS, enter it in the online worksheet and the software does the calculations and makes the charts! It's easy.

- Ask your company to begin geographic tracking
(Where do buyers come from? Keep these records by price range.)

Step II. Analyze the upper-tier market: Profile prospects

- Profile the upper-tier buyers & sellers in your market.
Are they corporate executives, second-home buyers, young high-techies, sports celebrities? What's the old money, new money mix? What do you think are their buying motivations? Which neighborhoods do they choose?

- Which categories or profile groups will you target? Why?
Rank the groups by opportunity level. Do you already have an entrée to any of these groups?
How should you position yourself?

- How can you begin to interact with your prospect groups?
Networking opportunities?

Step III. Analyze the upper-tier competition: Who's doing what?

- Identify players in upper price ranges –
which agents are your strongest competitors?

- What are their strengths & weaknesses?

- What affiliations and special upper-end programs do they have?

- How can you differentiate yourself?

- How can you network effectively?

Step IV. Line up your tools

Identify any special tools available from your network and/or company. Decide what other marketing resources you need.

Step V. Set some specific goals

How will you know you are making progress after 90 days? Six months? The first year?

What is your specific production goal for the first year?

Step VI. Develop a plan to market yourself and develop prospects

Remember there's no one right way to do this. Build on your strengths. How do you want to be positioned? What will differentiate you? Work on a positioning statement that clearly states in writing how you wish to be perceived in the luxury market. Build your self-promotion around that concept.

Your plan might start with some or all of these things...

- Volunteer to hold other agents'(or builders') listings open

- Send "we have listed, sold, or participated in the sale of" cards to the geographic areas or centers of influence you've targeted. You don't have to be the lister, but do coordinate with the lister/seller. He or she benefits, too! Be prepared to explain how.

- Create on-going market updates with the statistical info you've developed and mail them to your prospect groups. Provide information on market trends to the media, too. This is very important.

- Watch for business success stories and send article plus note and card.

- Develop networking relationships with country club membership managers, gate guards, architects, decorators, builders, and others who interact with the affluent. Develop a resource list for the affluent.

- Target move-ups. Work FSBOs and expireds in the price range just below the upper-tier or in the bottom of the upper-tier if your market offers that opportunity.

- Develop a personal brochure positioning you as an expert in the upper-price market.
- Have an Internet strategy for promoting yourself and your luxury properties.

Priorities Worksheet for Agents

Make a commitment to yourself to get to work now!

What are the FOUR most important things you can do now to begin or to expand your upper-tier business?

⇨**Priority No. 1:**

_____

Specific tasks/deadlines:

_____

_____

_____

_____ Deadline_____

Estimated cost: _____

⇨**Priority No. 2:**

_____

Specific tasks/deadlines:

_____

_____

_____

_____ Deadline_____

Estimated cost: _____

⇨Priority No. 3:

_____

Specific tasks / deadlines:

_____

_____

_____
_____ Deadline_____

Estimated cost: _____

⇨Priority No. 4:

_____

Specific tasks / deadlines:

Specific tasks / deadlines:

_____

_____

_____
_____ Deadline_____

Estimated cost: _____

In 60 days, I will be on track IF:

_____

_____

_____

_____

_____

Other ideas for getting started:

_____

_____

_____

_____

_____

NOTE: See Chapter 20 for an action plan for broker/owners and managers to use to build a luxury home program at the office or company level.

Chapter Eighteen
Trends in the luxury market

Demographics bode well for luxury niche

Increasingly, Realtors® recognize that demographics have a significant impact on total housing demand and the type of housing buyers purchase. Over the next two decades, we can expect some significant shifts in demand as a result of predicted demographic changes.

On one hand, new demand from the traditional homebuyers, married couples in their late 30s and early 40s with children, will decline as married households with children decline in numbers. On the other hand, demand sparked by single women, single men, empty-nest boomers and other non-traditional households is expected to grow.

These changes have already started. First time homebuyers are increasing as a percentage of total home purchasers as non-traditional buyers move into the marketplace. Single purchasers and unmarried couples already represent about 40 percent of all homebuyers.

Baby boomers (those born between 1946 and 1964) are primary drivers of home demand. As the youngest of the boomers continue to move into prime home buying years and progress in their careers (earning more), we should see a growing luxury home market. Affluent older boomers moving into their mid-fifties and early sixties may also fuel demand for move-up luxury homes, second homes, and retirement homes.

The product purchased is also beginning a subtle shift. Urban/center city and rural homes are increasing as a percentage of the total homes sold, while suburban purchases are slipping as a percentage of the total. Many expect this to continue as empty-nest boomers gravitate to new lifestyles, and other categories of childless buyers find urban lofts and other downtown residences attractive.

The accompanying charts, with their Census Bureau projections, may offer insight into overall housing demand and luxury home demand over the next two decades.

U.S. population projections by age group (in thousands)

Year	Total	Under 18	18-34	35-44	45-64	65 +
1995	262,820	68,743	65,789	42,514	52,231	33,543
2000	274,634	70,783	63,491	44,659	60,992	34,709
2005	285,981	71,963	64,574	42,165	71,113	36,166
2010	297,716	72,509	68,430	38,521	78,848	39,408
2020	322,742	77,603	72,853	39,612	79,454	53,220

Percentage change for 1995 to 2005

Total	Under 18	18-34	35-44	45-64	65 +
8.8%	4.7%	-1.9%	–	36%	7.8%

Percentage change from 1995 to 2020

Total	Under 18	18-34	35-44	45-64	65 +
22.8%	12.9%	10.7%	-6.8%	52%	58.6%

Source: U.S. Bureau of Census, Current Population Reports

Projected households by types, 1995 to 2010

	1995	2000	2005	2010	Change
Family Households*	68.4	71.7	74.7	77.9	13.9%
With Children	32.6	33.1	32.7	32.2	-1.2%
Without Children	35.8	38.6	42.0	45.7	27.7%
Single Households	24.3	26.2	28.3	30.7	26.3%
Other	5.0	5.4	5.8	6.2	24.0%
TOTAL	97.7	103.2	108.8	114.8	17.5%

* This category includes households of married couples and other households comprised of related family members.

Source: U.S. Bureau of the Census, Current Population Reports

Luxury Home Trends

Bigger homes, smaller lots. More square footage is the holy grail of today's buyers. Homebuyers want larger rooms and more rooms. Often this extra interior space comes at the expense of lot size. The footprint of the house is larger relative to the size of the lot. In most markets you can see this trend in action if you have exclusive neighborhoods where tear-downs occur. A home purchase will result in the old home being scraped off the lot and a new larger home being constructed. Even though the small house concept is widely discussed by architects and others, the luxury homebuyer is buying or building BIG.

Architectural design consistency. The new luxury homes being built today have more architectural design integrity. Instead of combining styles or putting a facade of a particular style on the front of a home and leaving the other sides style-less, builders are using architectural styles more consistently both outside and inside the home. There is also a trend toward using designs appropriate to the location. For instance, look for Spanish mission home designs rather than French chateaux in the desert.

Although Tuscan designs are popular most everywhere.

Home offices. The desire for a home office transcends price range. In the average-price home, the office may be a computer desk built into a bedroom or an office nook on the landing at the top of the stairs. In a luxury home, the office may be as elaborate as a wood paneled office suite with conference area, room for a staff person and office machines, kitchen facility, multiple phone lines, and fast Internet connections. If you're marketing a home without a home office, it's worth thinking about how existing space might be adapted for an office.

Housing moving to town. The concept of living and working in a downtown environment where you can walk to shopping and restaurants is catching on. Entire new town centers with retail, office, and residential spaces are springing up in suburban areas that never had downtowns. City developers are converting office or retail to residential lofts and building new townhouses and other residences downtown. Generally there is a mix of housing types and price ranges with the luxury home well represented.

This trend back to town still appears to be healthy in most markets. In fact, special subsidy programs in New York have helped to restore demand in the areas of lower Manhattan that were affected by the World Trade Center tragedy. Today, lower Manhattan is a hot residential area.

New Urbanism. Simplistically, New Urbanism is a reaction to suburban sprawl, a movement based on principles of planning and architecture that combine to create human-scale, walkable neighborhoods and communities. Hundreds of new towns, villages, and neighborhoods are planned or under construction in the U.S., using principles of the New Urbanism. Small-scale infill projects are underway, hoping to restore the urban fabric of communities by establishing a pedestrian environment. These projects combine a wide range of residential, retail, and commercial buildings and generally include luxury residences.

Concierge Services. Affluent individuals are accustomed to using the services of the concierge in a fine hotel. Dinner reservations, theatre tickets, limousine arrangements, and other services are available quickly and easily from the concierge. Increasingly, concierge services are being introduced in the luxury market. Luxury condominium and cooperative buildings offer concierge services similar to those of a hotel. Developers of luxury primary home communities and resort developments are offering concierge programs to residents. Even individual agents are getting into the act by providing expanded services to their clientele or by contracting with Concierge Service companies to offer concierge services to buyers and sellers.

Many brokerage firms have developed special customer service programs that may be labeled as concierge services but are often one-stop-shopping programs for homeownership services. For the affluent prospect, time is money and the ability to buy, obtain a mortgage, close, arrange homeowners' insurance, and have utilities connected all with a single point of contact is added value. If a brokerage also offers expanded homeownership services to include recommended vendors and coordination of things like pool and yard maintenance, home repair and renovation plus appliance discounts and other product and services savings, so much the better say many home buyers and sellers.

Ready-made mansions. A trend in high dollar home sales is the instant mansion—new homes that come furnished, decorated, and ready for occupancy. For the busy professional or the buyer who isn't confident about his or her own taste, a ready-made home is an easy solution. People who have multiple homes sometimes prefer this time-saving solution. Fully furnished units are also popular in the condo market, where this trend combines with the desire for luxury branded merchandise. Developers will offer several packages of furnishings and accessories put together by big name fashion designers like Armani.

Big city trends: instant penthouses and "building up". As demand for in-town housing grows in many markets, developers have had to get creative. When space in desirable buildings is fully utilized, "building-up" or the addition of an instant penthouse residence provides new income options for building owners or more space for owner/occupants.

First Penthouse Ltd., a Swedish company, specializes in ready-made penthouses that are installed on top of existing buildings. The company buys roof space, does the necessary preparation work for installation (electrical, plumbing, etc.) then builds the new penthouses in their Swedish factory. The exterior of each penthouse is designed and finished to match its host building. When completed, the penthouse is lifted into place by cranes and interior finish-out is done on site. The building owner shares in the profit. The firm has installed a number of residential units on top of London's historic Albert Court apartment building.

A similar concept involving penthouse additions is the onsite construction of a new top floor – referred to as "building up." The New York City condominium market is home to many new penthouses as a result of building owners' desires to offer new construction and spectacular city views while maximizing their buildings' revenue.

Big city trends: branded condominiums. Looking for ways to differentiate luxury condominium developments, developers first turned to big name architects and marketed the "signature" buildings they designed for a premium. Does the architect make a difference? A Michael Graves-designed building in Miami's trendy South Beach commanded a premium of about 20 percent more than comparable units in other buildings.

It's like putting Polo on a shirt. The Richard Meier-designed twin towers in New York City's Greenwich Village reported Calvin Klein and Martha Stewart as early buyers. Both snatched up penthouse units. Major cities, including New York and Chicago, hosted new buildings carrying names like Philip Johnson, Robert Stern, and Charles Gwathmey. Major developers like Donald Trump quickly got in the act with name-brand condominiums. Hotels joined the branding fray and hotel condo towers have sprung up bearing the Ritz Carlton, Mandarin Oriental, W, and other hotel brands. Fashion designers and fashion brands have now joined the branded condo trend.

Green and self sustaining developments. As concern about the environment grows, so too, does the movement toward "green" or ecologically friendly building and development. For example, Dockside Green in Victoria, British Columbia (Canada) is a new 1.3 million square foot mixed use development – the first community ever to target LEED Platinum certification for buildings developed in a master planned community. LEED is an independently audited, green building evaluation tool whereby points are awarded for energy and water efficiency, site ecology issues, indoor air quality, the use of environmental building materials and climate change initiatives. Only four buildings in the world have reached the platinum level.

The developers of Dockside Green reinforced their commitment to the environment with a potential penalty of up to $1 million dollars ($1 per buildable sq. ft.) payable to the city should they not obtain the LEED Platinum designation for each and every building in the development.

Manhattan's trendy Battery Park City is the site of The Visionaire, an "environmentally sensitive" 33 floor / 251 unit condominium tower featuring a high-efficiency fresh-air supply and exhaust system, centrally filtered water, an in-building wastewater treatment system that re-supplies toilets and provides water for central air-conditioning. Rainwater is harvested on the pesticide-free roof gardens.

Resort developers are going green as well. The Maui Land and Pineapple Company in Hawaii has combined a luxury residential and tourist resort with a 6000 acre working pineapple plantation and the largest private nature preserve in Hawaii. The resort's golf courses are even Audubon sanctuaries.

Fractional Ownership. Fractional ownership companies have moved into the luxury home market and are offering updated approaches to enjoying a vacation home while, at the same time, increasing the number of consumers who can afford a luxury lifestyle. Many of the players offering these new options for luxury homeownership are brands better known for offering other kinds of luxury products and services.

The Ritz-Carlton, Four Seasons, Starwood, and Marriott are major hotel brands which have moved into the condominium fractional ownership business by offering high end resort residences in desirable locations from Aspen or Jupiter Island to the Caribbean. The fractional or shared ownership model allows the buyer to use a particular property for a set period of time. These fractional companies are an increasingly upscale version of the old timeshare model. Consumers considering this approach to homeownership must be prepared to share property ownership with strangers and will be selling shares in the property when they are ready to end their ownership.

Vacation Clubs on the other hand, do not sell shares in particular properties, but offer memberships which allow participants the opportunity to choose from a group of deluxe properties – from fabulous homes to exclusive yachts – in an assortment of locations, for a defined length of time. This approach to ownership capitalizes on the well-heeled's desire to travel and to seek adventure and "experiences." Vacation club members can choose to vacation all around the world and have "their own" fabulous home in which to stay.

Clubs at the upper end – like Exclusive Resorts or Abercrombie and Kent have membership fees in the hundreds of thousands of dollars and may charge annual dues of $10,000 or more. Let your membership lapse, and the club will generally return a hefty portion of your initial membership fee. This business model maximizes variety and choice for the consumer. Smart shoppers will research the financial strength and management capabilities of the clubs which bear the risk and/or reap the benefits of changes in the real estate market. Most developers pay generous referral fees to agents for referred buyers. These fees are often equivalent to the fee on a traditional luxury sale.

While the fractional or vacation club models don't offer the same benefits of full ownership, they do allow the consumer to enjoy more home for the same investment. Resort buyers are flocking to these new resort home alternatives. Savvy Realtors® should understand the pros and cons of these new options, network with the providers, and be prepared to refer their clients who are interested in these opportunities.

Sporting Club Developments. More traditional luxury resort developers are differentiating their luxury projects by turning them into sporting clubs offering a broad range of sports. For example, the Greenbrier Sporting Club in West Virginia in addition to offering lots of luxury housing options, offers golf, tennis, horseback riding, fly fishing, skeet shooting, as well as more than 50 activities offered by the historic Greenbrier resort hotel and spa around which the development centers. Members may build or buy onsite. The developer, DPS Sporting Club Development, has numerous resorts with diverse sporting facilities aimed at the retiree or resort homeowner who wants to stay active. This type development also offers referral opportunities.

Chapter Nineteen

Just for Fun...
Insights based on Client Choices in Interior Design

There are many ways to segment the rich buyer and rich seller. In real estate, you can also often spot different affluent lifestyle groups by how their homes are decorated. Interior design choices of your clients can give you some interesting insight into motivations, attitudes, what will appeal to prospects, and how to sell them more effectively. Understanding these differences will also help you stage a home to appeal to a variety of different groups.

Here are some affluent lifestyle groups as defined by home decor. See if you recognize any of your clients and customers on this list. Do you recognize yourself? You may be able to add some other lifestyle groups. The important point is that lifestyles influence the types of homes people want and their choices in interior décor can often give you some insights into how to make your interactions with them more effective.

For those of you who are very visual, you'll have fun with the concept. Others of you will say, "What???" If that's you, just skip to the next chapter.

TRAVELERS

These folks love to travel and their excitement about the places they've been is reflected in their daily lives and in their homes. Their decorating is eclectic. A Moroccan table, an African mask,

Indian candlesticks, a rug from Santa Fe, and a Russian icon might accessorize the same room. They often use bright, spicy colors. Their approach to home design is not about fashion; it is about preserving the memories of their travels. They want a home that showcases their travel treasures. A custom home that has international design features may appeal to them. They may have multiple homes and be concerned about security when they travel. Letting them tell you their travel tales is a quick rapport builder. When you are out for the day showing travelers, take them to lunch at the most exotic ethnic restaurant in town.

FLAMBOYANTS

This group not only wants to be noticed, they want their wealth recognized. Their decorating will be lavish and extravagant. (Think gold bathroom fixtures.) They often gravitate to the trophy house with a long list of special amenities. Entertaining is important to them. They wear initialed brand clothing, drive luxury cars, drop names, and know what's hot and what's not. They can be great fun to have as clients. Dress up to work with this group. Show them your most flamboyant properties in the "best" neighborhoods. Plan lunch somewhere trendy where they can see and be seen.

SPARTANS

Keep it simple might be the mantra of the sophisticated Spartans. For this group, minimal is more. An urban loft or a sleek suburban contemporary may have great appeal. Good design and effective use of space is important. Don't show them anything too elaborate or cute. White, black, lots of glass, open floor plans, and large rooms, will appeal to this prospect type. Simplicity will carry over to how they dress. Don't take them to a tearoom for lunch—a sophisticated bistro would be better. The decor may be more important than the food.

ROMANTICS

At the opposite end of the spectrum from the Spartans are the romantics—we could call them the Martha Stewart set. Their homes are decorated in soft colors, with lots of romantic, feminine touches. They are family-oriented and warm. They want their home to be a luxurious, nurturing environment. Show them the "character house" -- the charming English Tudor, the white-columned colonial, or the sprawling beachfront family compound. Do go to the tearoom for lunch and ask to see the children or grandchildren's photos.

OUTDOOR LOVERS

These prospects love nature and bring it indoors. Their homes will incorporate natural materials like slate, stone, logs, and exposed wood. The view will matter to this group. Panoramic water or mountain views, settings in the woods, and other outdoor environments will appeal. This group is likely to have a second home in a beautiful locale. They are concerned about protecting the environment, will want to know if the neighborhood has recycling facilities, and may appreciate the home with grounds that have reverted to a natural state. Ask where they'd like to have a second or future retirement home and refer them. Take them to an upscale vegetarian restaurant for lunch or get gourmet carry out and eat in the park.

COLLECTORS

This is a small group, but easily recognized. These prospects are collectors and their home is the museum or showcase for their collection. They may collect paintings, antiques, sculpture, cars, or any number of other things, but whatever it is, they have a lot of it and it takes center stage in their homes. If possible, look at their collections to get a better sense of their needs. Match the homes to their display needs —lots of wall space for art, high ceilings and spacious rooms for large-scale antique furniture,

and so on. Take the time to learn a little about what they collect, ask a few intelligent questions, and they'll open up and tell
you more about their needs. Have lunch in the museum dining
room.

Once you have a feeling for the different styles, one way to use
them is to think about them when staging your listings. Can
you add a few accessories that say "traveler" to a spartan's
house and expand the appeal? Can you simplify a flamboyant's house just a bit and make it appeal to a romantic, too? You
can probably forget staging a flamboyant's home to appeal to a
Spartan. Get the idea?

Chapter Twenty

Action Plan for Brokers and Managers

Here's a checklist for broker/owners or managers who wish to increase their average sales price, improve profitability, recruit talented agents by building a luxury-home marketing program for their firm or office.

Getting Started
Why Develop a Luxury Home Program For Your Company or Office?

Business opportunity:

- The luxury market niche is growing (despite the generally slowing market)
- It is a segment that is reasonably resistant to economic changes
- Strategic approach to maintaining and increasing volume and revenue in an otherwise down market
- Upscale consumers prefer agents with access to special luxury programs
- Higher percentage of all cash transactions than "average priced properties"
- Opportunity to differentiate to attract a specific market segment with unique wants and needs

Recruiting and Retention Benefits:

- A luxury program allows you to attract and keep more successful real estate agents

Income/Profitability Benefits:

- Transaction size is larger
- Fees are higher

Analyze the Upper Tier Market (nationally and locally)

- National Market Statistics:
    - ◊ Percentage of total sales the luxury market represents
    - ◊ Number of million dollar home sales annually
    - ◊ Other national luxury market stats
- Local Market Statistics:
    - ◊ Analyze your luxury market by price bands
    - ◊ Use your "price band analysis" to find opportunities

Analyze Your Competitive Situation

Competitive Analysis: Research on the competition

- Who are your competitors (firms) in the luxury market?
- Don't assume you know, do an analysis of MLS data
- How much market share do they control in each price range?
- What are the characteristics of their luxury programs
- What are their luxury program strengths and weaknesses?
- How might you position your firm's luxury program as unique and better?

Key Steps in Developing Your Program

Step 1. Management Must Commit To Building a Luxury Brand

- Top Management must view it as a priority and commit necessary funds

- Sales managers must "buy-in"

- There must be a Program Manager to "drive" the program

- There must an internal plan to capture agent "buy-in" and participation

- Understand the factors necessary in budgeting for your program

Step 2. Establish Clear Policies and Systems

- Define Your Upper-Tier Market
  (What property price point will you use?)
  - ◊ Price definition should be specific to your marketplace

  - ◊ Two common approaches: Multiples of average or median price or certain percentage of the market's sales (such as top 10% of sales based on price)

  - ◊ Define the geographic area your program will cover

- Define Property Requirements
  (Will you establish requirements for properties in addition to price?)
  - ◊ Define types of residences your program will include

  - ◊ (single family, condo, co-op, duplex?)

  - ◊ Clarify quality standards for homes

  - ◊ Will you accept single family zoned lots which meet price requirement?
    (What other special situations will you need to plan for)

- Decide if your program will be agent-oriented or property-oriented

    ◊ Decide if any luxury property which meets requirements may be placed in program or if listing agent must qualify before a property can be part of program or will you have combination of both? Policies must be clear!

    ◊ Create policy manual for your luxury program

Step 3. Develop a Marketing Plan for Your Luxury Program

- Choose a name for your program

    ◊ Make it memorable, clearly associated with the luxury home segment, and unlike competitors' program names

- Create a roll-out campaign for your program

    ◊ How will you roll-out your program internally to generate buy-in and participation?

    ◊ How will you roll-out the program in the marketplace?

    ◊ How can you use the media to create visibility for the roll-out?

- Determine how you will package, position, and promote your program on an ongoing basis

    ◊ Have clear marketing goals and a specific marketing budget

    ◊ Use PR to leverage your program's exposure

Step 4. Create Your Basic Package of Tools

- Determine what materials you need and set development priorities

    ◊ Create general consumer-oriented materials for the luxury program: general brochure, section on website, institutional ads, downloadable logos and logo use guidelines, etc.

    ◊ Create agent promotional materials: folder, letterhead, note cards, business cards, etc.

◊ Create property marketing materials: yard signage, property brochure formats, just listed/just sold cards, property specific website formats, etc.

Step 5. Build Marketing Partnerships and Incorporate Special Resources

- Decide which service and product providers you want to use

  ◊ Add value to your program with additional products and services for consumers and your agents

  ◊ Establish preferred vendor relationships and negotiate special discounts

Step 6. Train Your Agents and Give Them Important Credibility (They deliver the service!)

- Maximize the probability that luxury consumers will view your agents as unique and better able to meet their needs

  ◊ Be sure your agents have the competencies they need to succeed – In this market segment it is NOT about whom you know, it is about what you know

  ◊ Research says luxury buyers and sellers are looking for agents with market knowledge and a luxury designation. Arm your agents with both.

  ◊ Select a luxury training program and designation and incorporate into your luxury program

Step 7. Understand What Your Agents Must Know To Be Successful (This information will also help you design your Luxury Home Program)

- Who are the buyers and sellers of luxury homes?

- What are luxury homebuyers and sellers' needs and expectations?

- How do they select real estate agents?
- What detailed luxury home market knowledge must one have?
- What special competencies over and above those of other agents must one develop?

Step 8. Know How You Will Measure Your Luxury Program's Success

- Establish specific, measurable goals for your program

Chapter Twenty One
Canadian Statistics, eh?

Canadian median and mean family earnings

According to the Survey of Labour and Income Dynamics, in 2005, the median (after tax) household income in Canada for families comprised of two or more people was $56,000 (in Canadian dollars). The average or mean pre-tax income for these families was $78,400 (in Canadian dollars).

Statistics Canada reports on their Website (www.statcan.ca) that of the approximately 7.5 million Canadians, 1.8 million earned $100,000 or more in pretax income in 2005, while 156,490 of those are reported to have earned $250,000 or more before taxes.

Note that this is an apples-to-oranges comparison with U.S. household income which looks at households rather than at families of two or more.

Canadian income data is available broken down by letter carrier routes, census tracts, urban forward sortation areas (the first three characters of the postal code), cities, towns, federal electoral districts, census divisions, census metropolitan areas, economic regions, provinces, and territories. For more information, visit www.statcan.ca.

A look at Canada's wealthy

Canadian luxury home buyers resemble their counterparts from the states – they made their own fortunes by what they describe as "hard work."

A new survey conducted by Ipsos Reid on behalf of Royal LePage Realtors® finds that just 3% of wealthy homeowners have come from affluent families. Conversely, almost all (93%) wealthy homeowners, with an estimated real estate value of $500,000 or more, have come from "middle class" backgrounds. Interestingly, 4% of these homeowners have risen out of poverty and now enjoy the luxury of a home worth at least $500,000. In fact, many of these affluent homeowners don't just own one house. Nearly four in ten (36%) claim to have at least two homes, counting their primary residence.

When it comes to the value of primary residences, 12% of affluent Canadians live in homes with price tags starting at $1 million, while almost half (47%) of affluent respondents live in properties valued from $600,000 to $999,000. Well heeled Canadians seem a bit more willing to invest in luxury homes than their counterparts down south.

"Prosperous Canadians see real estate as an important element in their investment portfolios, according to Phil Soper, president and CEO, Royal LePage Real Estate Services. Demand for well-appointed properties remains strong with a trend of affluent Canadians owning more than one home. In fact, one-quarter of wealthy homeowners own two properties, and six per cent own three residences, while two per cent own more than five properties."

Many of these prosperous Canadians are boomers. As a group,

boomers represent one-third of Canada's population, but control 45% of its wealth. Boomers own $230 billion in real estate and their net worth totals $530 billion.

One trend to watch is boomers' acquisitions of second homes – recreation property sales are strong. Boomers are buying to enjoy and with an eye to the future. Many hope to use vacation retreats for family gatherings and also plan to pass these homes on to children or grandchildren. While investment may not be the first priority, recent appreciation in the resort and vacation segment has spurred purchases.

As of the first quarter of 2007, the urban luxury market was also alive and well across Canada. Upscale property sales were up from Montreal to Vancouver as compared to the first quarter of 2006.

Canadian Metro Market Luxury Home Statistics
1st Quarter 2007

Market	Price	Units Sold Q1 2007	Units Sold Q1 2006	% Change
Halifax	$600,000 +	8	10	-20%
Montreal	$900,000 +	56	49	14%
Ottawa	$750,000 +	23	7	229%
Toronto*	$1,000,000 +	434	357	22%
Winnipeg	$500,000 +	11	8	38%
Calgary	$1,000,000 +	130	94	38%
Edmonton	$950,000 +	12	7	71%
Vancouver*	$1,000,000 +	673	544	24%

* Greater metropolitan areas. Source: local real estate boards (TREB, CREB, WREB, REBGV, OREB, NSAR and Royal LePage)

General market information: According to the fourth installment of the 14th Annual RBC Homeownership Survey, conducted by Ipsos Reid, there is increased momentum in downsizing with 33% of potential homebuyers looking for a smaller home (versus 20% in 2006). This trend appears to be a result of the aging population and/or the Boomer movement: 37% of those 55+ are looking for a smaller home and 15% of this same group is considering a condo (compared to 10% overall).

Survey results also reveal that 37% of Canadian homeowners 55+ currently have a mortgage on their home and, on average; they have $80,331 left to pay.

Canada's Millionaires

Research indicates that Canada has at least 350,000 traditional millionaires. These are defined as those who, when you subtract liabilities from assets, have a net of $1million or more. These millionaires are concentrated in five provinces with Ontario home to more millionaires than any other province.

Canadian Millionaires By Level of Wealth, 2005

Number of millionaires	350,000
Mass millionnaires ($1M - $5M)	310,000
Penta-millionnaires ($5M - $10M)	47,000
Deca-millionnaires ($10M+)	18,000

Source: The Taddingstone Report

Geographic Distribution of Canadian Millionaires, 2005

Province	Number of Millionaires
British Columbia	65,000
Alberta	50,000
Ontario	160,000
Quebec	70,000
Rest of Canada	30,000

Source: The Taddingstone Report

Canada's High Net Worth Individuals (HNWI)

According to Merrill Lynch and CapGemni's *World Wealth Report, 2006*, Canada has 232,000 High Net Worth Individuals (HNWI), a number which is up over the previous year's report by 7.2%. This group is defined as those who have at least $1 million dollars (U.S) in investable assets, excluding principal residence. These individuals are sometimes referred to as "money millionaires" and certainly qualify for the ranks of the wealthy.

Where has their wealth come from? They've made their own money. Earned-income and business ownership (or sale of a business) has added the most to their assets.

Some of these HNWI are *über* rich. They have at least $30 million (U.S.) in investable assets. Twenty-three of them are among the world's 946 billionaires (according to Forbes' 2007 Billionaires Report). While the world's billionaires had a total net worth of $3.5 trillion. Canada's share of the billionaire treasure chest was $84 billion.

Canadian Business magazine also tracks the richest 100 Canadians and identified the three billionaires at the top of the list: the Thomson family of media fame ($24.4 billion); grocery mogul Galen Weston and his family ($7.1 billion); and the Irving family, known for their oil empire in Atlantic Canada ($5.45 billion).

Challenges for wealthy may create opportunities for you

Wealth doesn't solve all problems. A study done by Sensus Research, querying Canadians worth more than $10 million, found that almost 24% worry that their children or grandchildren will squander their inheritance. And about a third worry they won't be able to maintain their own lifestyle. Those millions just don't go as far as they used to! The wealthy in Canada today do have to deal with many issues, some of which will have an impact on their real estate decisions:

The sandwich generation: According to Statistics Canada, 70% of baby boomers – and hence many millionaires – expect to have to look after both adult children and aging parents, leaving them less time for other activities. This may also change their housing needs. Mother-in-law apartments as part of or adjacent to primary residences or condos for more independent parents may be on the shopping list of affluent households.

Cross border complexity: Many wealthy Canadians live and work in multiple places with differing and constantly changing laws and regulations. They may need professional help with real estate in multiple countries and also need the corollary services – from tax and legal advice to financial services and perhaps translation assistance. Networking with other service providers internationally makes sense.

Time to retire and cash in: A recent study by the Canadian Federation of Independent Business says almost half of small and medium-sized business owners (and there are a lot of them) intend to retire within the next five years. Yet only a small percentage of these potential millionaires actually have a formal succession or sales plan. Those who do make a successful transition will most like have money to spend on a retirement or vacation home.

The will: Canadian boomers may be inheriting money from their WWII generation parents, but their children are starting to inherit as well. Some of this money will be earmarked for moving up or buying another house.

These challenges present opportunities for the real estate professional who takes the time to understand the needs and expectation of wealthy Canadians.

Chapter Twenty Two
About The Institute for Luxury Home Marketing

Real estate professionals around the globe who want to maximize their success in the luxury home market turn to The Institute for Luxury Home Marketing (ILHM), the authority in training and certifying real estate professionals in the art of handling exceptional properties. The Institute awards the prestigious *Certified Luxury Home Marketing Specialist (CLHMS)* designation which is the official designation for a number of international real estate brands as well as for numerous regional and local residential brokerage companies. Members of The Institute who have earned the *CLHMS* designation and have track records of success in the million dollar plus market segment, can also earn The Institute's *Million Dollar Guild* recognition which gives them added credibility in their markets.

The Institute's mission is to help real estate professionals deliver quality service to the buyers and sellers of luxury properties and in so doing, maximize their own success. To help accomplish this goal, the Institute has four key areas of focus:

1. Providing information and helping build agents' luxury market competencies. *The Certified Luxury Home Marketing Specialist* designation training – which all members receive – helps agents better understand the motivations and expectations of the luxury consumer and helps fine-tune the special competencies agents need to work successfully in the luxury home market. As of the writing of this book, The Institute's two-day certification training has been approved for two elective credits toward the National Association of Realtor's *Certified Residential Specialist (CRS)* designation. The Institute also offers a course on developing a luxury home program for broker/owners and office managers. This day-long session provides an elective credit toward earning NAR's *Certified Residential Broker (CRB)* designation.

2. Serving real estate professionals as a resource for research and market data. The Institute provides its members with access to the knowledge and information needed to be successful in an ever-changing market by supplying luxury home market data as well as primary and secondary research information on the demographic and psychographic characteristics of affluent buyers and sellers. This keeps members up-to-speed on questions such as: Who are the best prospects? How do you find them? What are their expectations? How do they choose their real estate professionals? How can you deliver the services that meet their objectives and result in repeat business and referrals?

3. Helping agents brand themselves as luxury home experts. The Institute works to position its members as the real estate professionals of choice for affluent consumers who wish to work with sales professionals who have credibility and special competencies in the listing and selling of fine homes and estate properties. The Institute also provides its members with special marketing tools to help brand themselves as luxury home experts. Members also benefit from special discounts and value added services offered by The Institute's marketing partners.

4. Creating an international network of luxury home experts. Dedicated to building an international membership base of sales professionals, The Institute is constantly working to build a strong network of luxury specialists around the world. This network is a source of the best ideas and business practices in luxury home marketing, as well as a resource for referrals. The Institute has thousands of members on four continents.

If you are a real estate professional who would like more information on the training and certification available through The Institute, please contact The Institute at +1 (214) 485-3000, or by email at info@luxuryhomemarketing.com. You can also visit us on the web at www.luxuryhomemarketing.com. You can find our *Luxury Insights* blog at: http://blog.luxuryhomemarketing.com.

About the author

Laurie Moore-Moore

The Chicago Tribune calls Laurie Moore-Moore "The Luxury Real Estate Diva." *Unique Homes* magazine selected her as one of the "35 Most Influential People in the Luxury Home Market Today."

The Real Estate Intelligence Report declared she is one of the ten people having the most impact on U.S. residential real estate in the last 25 years.

Known for her expertise on the affluent consumer, Laurie is quoted in publications as varied as the Wall Street Journal, USA Today, The Chicago Tribune, and The Washington Post. She has personally trained over 12,000 agents in the marketing of luxury homes.

Laurie is Founder and CEO of The Institute for Luxury Home Marketing, an organization founded in 2003, with thousands of members on four continents. The Institute awards the international *Certified Luxury Home Marketing Specialist* designation for real estate professionals who successfully market upscale residential properties.

Laurie is the co-founder and former co-editor of REAL *Trends*, a major real estate industry research and communications company.

She has sold real estate, managed a real estate office, and run two divisions of one of the nation's largest real estate firms.

Laurie is a member of the board of directors of a Fortune 1000 company.